CRISIS IN CHUBUT

CRISIS IN CHUBUT

*A chapter in the history of the Welsh
Colony in Patagonia*

GERAINT DYFNALLT OWEN

Christopher Davies
Swansea

To
Karin and John

© Geraint Dyfnallt Owen
Published in 1977 by
Christopher Davies (Publishers) Ltd
4/5 Thomas Row
Swansea SA1 1NJ

ISBN 0 7154 0127 0

*Printed in Wales by
Salesbury Press Ltd
Llandybie, Dyfed*

CONTENTS

PREFACE

The title of this book was the subject of a lecture delivered at the University College of Wales, Aberystwyth, early in 1969. Later research into unpublished material relating to the history of the Welsh colonists in Patagonia produced further evidence that the desire of many of them to resettle under British administration was strong enough to initiate a number of projects for their removal at the beginning of the present century.

My thanks are due to the staffs of the Public Record Office and the National Library of Wales for their kind assistance over the years. I am also very grateful to Mrs. A. E. Gell, of Hopton Hall, Derbyshire, for permitting me to consult and quote from the papers and correspondence of the late Philip Lyttelton Gell.

Geraint Dyfnallt Owen

PART 1

Struggle and Disillusionment

The seeds of the crisis that was to threaten the Welsh colony in Patagonia with disintegration at the beginning of this century had been laid before any of the settlers set foot on the territory of Chubut in 1865.

Rarely had a scheme for colonization been launched in circumstances which were liable sooner or later to generate serious economic and political difficulties. The promoters of the enterprise could, perhaps, have hardly foreseen them. Nevertheless, they cannot be entirely exonerated from a sad neglect in not assessing, as correctly as was possible at the time, the actual situation in Patagonia before dispatching 150 of their countrymen to an isolated valley in that immense and practically unexplored land.

For instance, they might have inquired why an attempt by the Argentine Government itself to plant a colony at Chubut eleven years previously had proved a dismal failure. In that case, was it likely that a handful of Welshmen, however courageous and determined, would succeed where Argentine pioneers had given up the struggle? If Michael D. Jones, the eminent Principal of Bala College and a leading figure in the Welsh Emigration Society, and his colleagues were aware of this abortive venture, they did not allow themselves to be discouraged by it. What is more questionable, however, was their decision to proceed with the project when they must have known of the conflict of opinion among Argentine political circles as to the desirability of a foreign settlement in Patagonia and a - to them - English one at that.

Two years before, in 1863, when the Welsh Emigration Society had approached the Argentine Government with a proposal to found a colony at Chubut, the idea had been warmly welcomed. Senor Rawson, the Minister of the Interior, was enthusiastic, and the Project of Law, formulated by the Government and which embodied the conditions of settlement, was highly advantageous to the prospective settlers. There were liberal grants of land and gifts of stock, the colonists were exempted from all military obligations for ten years, and a wide measure of local autonomy was conceded. Further rights and privileges were envisaged as the settlement developed, and the Emigration Society was sufficiently elated to undertake to send between 300 and 500 emigrants annually to Patagonia for the next ten years. (1)

That the Argentine Minister of the Interior was sincere and accommodating needed no further evidence. But what the Emigration Society, and possibly Senor Rawson himself, had not anticipated was an eruption of anti-English feeling in the Legislative Assembly of the Argentine Republic, the Congress, which rejected outright the Project of Law when it was submitted for its approval. The principal objection voiced by Congress was the proximity of the proposed colony to the Falkland Islands. Britain's occupation of the Islands was a constant irritant to public opinion in Buenos Aires, and the Argentine Government itself held tenaciously to its claim that the grant of independence extracted from Spain by the Republic, earlier in the nineteenth century, had included the surrender of Spanish sovereignty over the Falkland Islands. The Government was circumspect and discreet in the matter, but not so the militant elements in Congress. They were dedicated to the notion that wherever British colonists managed to establish themselves, the British Government would eventually yield to an irresistible urge to claim their territory as inalienably British. Their fears were apparently excited by the thought that the presence of Welsh settlers in Patagonia would whet expansionist appetites in London and the Falkland Islands.

The opposition in Congress could hardly have been more inopportune to Senor Rawson. A man of outstanding perspicacity at a time when Argentine politics were actuated by provincial and personal interests and jealousies, he had realized for some time that the Argentine's assumption of sovereignty over Patagonia was open to one serious objection. This was the simple physical fact that Patagonia was not occupied by the country that claimed to possess it. For all practical purposes the southern boundary of the Argentine lay along the Rio Negro. Beyond that river stretched the un-surveyed land of Patagonia tenanted solely by wandering Indian tribes. In Senor Rawson's view there was only one valid and recognized method of establishing Argentine suzerainty, the organization of settlements under the authority and protection of the Republic. The Minister made no attempt to conceal his convictions on this point, even from the British Minister in Buenos Aires, who informed his Government that, "a settlement formed under its (the Argentine's) sanction and protection would, he (Rawson) considered, put at rest the question of the somewhat undefined sovereignty over those remote and uncivilized regions." (2)

In 1863 some operation of this nature had become imperative. Congress's apprehensions of alleged British annexationist manoeuvres could be discounted. Any opposition from the Indians could be treated with contempt. What Senor Rawson and his Government could not ignore was the attitude and activities of their western neighbour, Chile. That country had already groped its way southwards to the Straits of Magellan, and claimed them to be an integral part of its national territory. Now it was putting forward more disturbing pretensions to sovereignty over Patagonia as far north as Rio Negro. It was an extravagant claim, and probably meant to be exploited as a bargaining point or as a concession in return for the recognition of Chile's possession of the Straits. Whatever the object, it called for some demonstration on the part of the Argentine of her ability to justify and enforce her sovereign rights over Patagonia.

To forestall a possible colonizing drive eastwards by Chile was the obvious solution, and a settlement of Welshmen could be as effectual a countermeasure as any other. Undeterred by the lack of cooperation from Congress, Senor Rawson stuck to his scheme and prosecuted it by all available means. He even - rather inadvisedly - tried to make a deal with the British Government on the delicate matter of the Falkland Islands. In a conversation with Thornton, the British Minister in Buenos Aires, he spoke of the necessity of conciliating Congress and asked, "whether Her Majesty's Government would not be disposed to take into consideration the possibility of the Islands being ceded to the Argentine Republic, adding that if it were in his power to put forward this prospect Congress, he was convinced, would put no obstacle in the way of the original contract with the Welsh Committee being carried out." (3) Thornton was courteous but returned the uncompromising answer that his Government would not contemplate the cession of the Falkland Islands for a single moment.

It is difficult to conceive that Rawson really expected the British Government to entertain the notion of exchanging a group of islands of strategic importance to its naval and merchant shipping for an assurance that a few Welshmen should be allowed to settle peacefully in an inaccessible Patagonian valley. But with Chile's claims ringing in his ears, he was determined to get them there. Eventually a loophole was found in a piece of Congress legislation which Rawson skilfully turned to account. In 1862 a Land Bill had been passed regulating the conditions under which immigrants could receive and hold Government lands, and granting 100 acres to every three adults. This concession was made the basis of a new agreement with the Emigration Society in Wales.

In the light of subsequent events, there is some evidence that the Society acted too precipitately in accepting this concession as an adequate provision for the initial stage in the establishment of the colony. It was made clear to them by the Argentine Consul at Liverpool in a letter of November 22, 1864, that no further facilities or inducements could be extended for the moment. Nevertheless, the Society acted as if its members were confident of more substantial Government aid, and that what had been covenanted in the rejected Project of Law would be implemented in due course. They could have committed no greater error. Even the prospectus which they issued, with the exception of the grant of 100 acres, must have appeared uncomfortably vague except to those who had irrevocably made up their minds to leave Wales.

By May 31, 1865, one hundred and fifty men, women and children were assembled on board the *Mimosa,* due to sail from Liverpool that day. They had seven thousand miles of ocean and forty miles of waterless land to cross before reaching the Chubut valley. Since the journey would take two months at least, and the season for planting seed in that part of Patagonia was from May to June, they would arrive at their destination with no prospect of a harvest for a whole year. How they were to maintain themselves until the time came for tilling and sowing the virgin soil of Chubut was a question which does not appear to have been thoroughly examined by the Welsh Emigration Committee. Yet one member was genuinely troubled by a premonition that the unknown land of Patagonia might have problems in store for the unsuspecting emigrants. Whatever his views on the English "Establishment" in Wales, Michael D. Jones thought it desirable that a British warship should visit the colony occasionally to see how it was progressing. (4)

The *Mimosa* arrived at Bahia Nueva on July 28. A number of children had died during the voyage but others had been born, and most of the Welshmen who set foot on dry land that day were in good spirits. It was when they began to grapple with the problem of transporting themselves to the Chubut valley that the gravity of their situation and the insufficiency of their resources dawned on them. After weeks of enforced delay most of the men made their way overland through an arid waste, where intolerable thirst would sometimes force a man to resort to an obnoxious way of allaying it. The women and children were taken by sea in the schooner *Mary Ellen* and experienced much misery and near starvation. It was October before the settlers reached Chubut, and still later in the year when they were allocated their respective holdings.

Such, however, was the deplorable lack of even the elementary necessities of life that there was a real danger of the colony succumbing to starvation during the first weeks of its existence. A desperate move by Lewis Jones, the most resourceful and undoubtedly the most prominent member of the community, to relieve the situation by drawing bills on England without sanction did little to help. Discontent, uncertainty and a feeling of impotence combined to breach the cohesion which had held the Welsh together. An appeal, allegedly signed by nineteen of the settlers, was sent to the Governor of the Falkland Islands, urging him to take immediate steps to save the signatories from their wretched situation. It was communicated to London where it awoke the British Government to the inescapable fact that the fate of the Welsh in Patagonia was a matter that concerned it deeply, and was likely to do so for some time to come.

While the Foreign Office was pondering over the message, Senor Rawson was acting with decision and expedition. He lost no time in assessing the predicament and needs of the isolated and hungry colonists. True he had been disconcerted by the improvident manner in which the emigration had been organized in Wales. He had been led to believe that the first contingent would consist of experienced labourers or better class farmers equipped with agricultural implements and seed. Instead, he found a band of hardy but strangely assorted settlers, very few of whom possessed any knowledge of farming.

This was, perhaps, the least pressing of the problems that confronted Senor Rawson. The cardinal objective, as he conceived it, was to preserve the colony at all costs, and prevent any tendency towards its abandonment. Already there were rumours that some of the Welsh were seriously considering a move to Rio Negro, where they could find employment on the extensive estates in that region. For others there were better prospects in the urban communities near the same river. Rawson had little doubt that once the colony was dispersed, there was little likelihood that other emigrants would be attracted to Patagonia. Consequently his scheme of colonization would be indefinitely postponed.

It was a contingency to which he reacted with a vigour and determination which may have outrun financial discretion, but which certainly saved the colony from extinction. He procured a monthly subsistence allowance of £140 to ensure a constant supply of provisions, besides a supplementary grant for the purchase of live stock. Another £200 was set aside to compensate the native Indians for the tribal lands allotted to the Welsh. These sums were deducted from a Government fund of £4000 earmarked for the encouragement of colonization within the Republic. That Senor Rawson was prepared to exceed that sum in order to keep the Chubut colony on its feet reflected his sincere belief that to allow it to expire for want of assistance, even sacrifice, on the part of the Government, was detrimental to the interests of the Argentine.

The British Chargé d'Affaires in Buenos Aires, who compiled the first official report on the colony for his Government, was emphatic that it would not have survived without Rawson's intervention and aid. "Nevertheless," he added, "it should not be lost sight of that in a political point of view the (Argentine) Government have had an object in making a sacrifice to promote the settlement of a colony at any cost under the flag of the Republic on Patagonian soil which they claim as Argentine territory, but which, from its hitherto unoccupied condition has been open to dispute, although no direct question as to its rightful sovereignty has been pressed upon the Government." (6) Senor Rawson's resoluteness in upholding his country's claims to Patagonia were not of particular interest to the British Government, which repeatedly expressed its complete detachment from the conflicting pretensions of Chile and the Argentine. But it was impressed by the solicitude shown by him, and by the alacrity with which he had responded to the sufferings and destitution of the Welsh. Ford, the Chargé d'Affaires, was notified in due course that the Secretary for Foreign Affairs, the Earl of Clarendon, considered "the conduct of Senor Rawson towards the colonists to have been both liberal and humane." (7)

However, serious doubts were expressed in London and Buenos Aires that the exposure of the colonists to the unpredictable hazards of a pioneer's life in Patagonia would prove too much for them. The secretary of the British Legation was directed to visit Chubut and investigate conditions for himself. His report, although not entirely favourable, scotched certain gloomy predictions. There was no sign of starvation, nor, for that matter, had there been any excuse for the frantic appeal to the Governor of the Falkland Islands. An inquiry revealed that the nineteen signatures appended to it had included the names of five children and others who had not been consulted. Still, heads were shaken in Whitehall when the report also disclosed that the colonists had only three ploughs between them to till the soil, and that without the monthly allowance from Buenos Aires the settlement would virtually cease to exist. (8).

There was no reason to question that statement, and there were occasions when the continuance of the colony hung in the balance as the Argentine Government periodically debated with itself whether further financing of the colony was justified. At one time it seemed that the Welsh would be removed *en masse* and offered land in the province of Santa Fé. The chronic failure of crops and the scarcity of food daunted even the most tenacious of the settlers, and in June, 1867, the whole community destroyed their homes, slaughtered most of their cattle and removed their remaining possessions to Guelfo Novo to await embarkation to the Chaco Lands in Santa Fé. After two months of indecisive negotiations in Buenos Aires, they returned to rebuild their houses in Chubut, and the arrival of Government stores helped them to weather the crisis and redirect their energies to the cultivation of the land. (9)

There is little doubt that it was the persuasive arguments of Lewis Jones, and the news of the impending arrival of a further group of Welsh emigrants, that swayed the Argentine Government into hastening to the rescue of the despairing colonists. But there were limits to the sympathy and indulgence of the authorities. In June, 1867, they agreed to postpone a final decision on the future of the colony, and to subsidize it, for another twelve months. (10) After that, it would be a matter for the Welsh to wean themselves from Government assistance or abide by the consequences, which for the time being were allowed to be conjectural. The warning was driven home by an event which must have dismayed the colonists. In 1868, Senor Rawson resigned as Minister of the Interior. The man who had done so much to inculcate amongst them a genuine attachment to Chubut no longer represented their interests and aspirations in Buenos Aires. The settlers did not forget the inestimable services which he had rendered them, and the town of Tre Rawson is a reminder of his close association with the colony during its formative years.

The more percipient members of the community had already realized that one of the basic problems facing them was the establishment of communications between Chubut and the outside world. If they were to supplement their limited resources with provisions purchased elsewhere, and pay for them with agricultural produce or whatever other exportable commodities were available, then there had to be a breakdown of the isolation in which the colony was entrapped. The difficulties which hampered overland contacts appeared insurmountable. Roads were non-existent and a waterless territory surrounded the settlement for hundreds of miles. Besides, the Welsh were at first disinclined to venture very far beyond the confines of the Chubut valley. There remained the sea, but even here there were dangers, inasmuch as there were few safe anchorages in the vicinity. Nevertheless, it presented the sole alternative to the complete segregation of the settlers, and their exposure to famine should crops continue to fail.

The fear of being cut off from people and events intensified from 1868 onwards, and there was little the settlers could do to improve the situation. It was their misfortune to be engaged in colonizing a remote corner of a Republic that was experiencing recurrent crises in its domestic and external affairs, and struggling against moral and financial bankruptcy.

The alliance of the Argentine with Uruguay and Brazil against Paraguay in 1865 had plunged the country into an exhaustive and protracted war, and cost millions of pounds which were sorely needed in other departments of the national life. (11) Unfortunately the end of the war aggravated rather than dissipated tension within the Republic. Disputes with its former allies over claims to Paraguayan territory precluded demobilization. A recrudescence of the conflict between the central Government in Buenos Aires and the provincial administrations resulted in sanguinary insurrections.

Concurrently with this challenge to legally constituted government a wave of outrages and murders swept through the Argentine Republic, bringing both law and judges into disrepute because of the impunity with which criminals escaped punishment. The situation became so bad that the *Standard,* the English language newspaper circulating in the capital, commented gloomily that "the progress of the land is in murder and immorality." (12) The British Chargé d'Affaires, MacDonnell, frustrated by his impotence in obtaining redress for British people who were victims of the disorders, could visualize no better practical method of dealing with the murderers but that of lynching them on the spot. (13).

It was not only with internal revolt and the threatening collapse of law and order amongst the white population that the Government had to contend. Taking advantage of the confusion and the withdrawal of frontier guards to fight in the Paraguayan war, the Indian tribes of the interior launched massive raids on the unprotected settlements in the provinces of Santa Fé and Cordoba. Not even the province of Buenos Aires was immune from these attacks, in which cattle and horses were stolen, settlers killed and hundreds of women and children taken into captivity. The futility of curbing the Indians, let alone of driving them back, seems to have been accepted by Government and citizens alike, and was reflected in the opinion of one Argentine paper that "to undertake the subjection of the Indians by force of arms is to undertake an enterprise impossible of realization." (14) From now on, as far as the Indians were concerned, the Government was content to remain on the defensive, and even to reconcile itself to the temporary surrender of its control over the immense tract of land between the Rio Negro and Chubut.

In Britain, the news of the precarious situation in the Republic led not only to a divergence of public opinion as to whether the Argentine was a safe place for Britons to seek their fortunes, but to official discouragement of emigration to that country. (15) In Chubut itself, arguments and advice were irrelevant. The isolation of the colony had been transformed by events into unpleasant reality. In June, 1869, the monthly supplies from Buenos Aires were abruptly suspended, and for twenty months the settlers were almost completely cut off from all contacts by land and sea, and thrown on their own resources. A small number decided to leave in August that year, and established themselves in the province of Santa Fé, but the majority of the Welsh preferred to grapple with a stubborn soil for a bare existence.

Their comparative success was primarily due to their real-istic appraisal of what the chances of survival meant in terms of personal relationships and communal effort. Unremitting physical work was, of course, a necessity; but so was an avoidance of dissensions which might hinder the community from acting as an unit. Authority was therefore vested in a democratically elected committee of twelve who regulated the affairs of the colony, and secured conformity and obedience from all without question. Complaints and transgressions were examined by a Justice of the Peace, supported by a jury if necessary, and a gaol was never required in Chubut while the colony was self-governing. Common sense prevailed in matters affecting the marital exigencies of a small community whose growth, always threatened by defections, depended on the fertility of a restricted number of females. Early marriages were regarded as desirable from all points of view, and it became the custom for girls to marry at the age of 14 or 15.

But nowhere did the colonists display greater shrewdness and humanity than in their relations with the Indians of Patagonia. At the outbreak of the Indian troubles in 1868, the Government had seen fit to provide the Welsh with rifles and ammunition, and to instruct them in the organization of a militia. The weapons were never used except for hunting. Strong ties of friendship developed between the Patagonian Indians and the Welsh, (16) which were not wholly commendable in the eyes of the Argentine Government, but which materially benefited the colonists when their position seemed untenable. It was the Indians who taught the new-comers to turn to hunting for their subsistence; it was, above all, their willingness to trade that provided the colonists with the more exotic of their exports to Buenos Aires - the feathers and skins of the pampas. That it was not thought requisite to build a single work of defence in Chubut, at a time when predatory Indians were murdering and looting in the north near Bahia Blanca, indicated the extraordinary degree of trust reposed by the Welsh in their primitive neighbours. In fact, the only danger that they had to face from that quarter was the possibility of contracting smallpox, whooping cough or some other ailment which afflicted the Indians.

In March, 1871, the British Legation in Buenos Aires, alarmed by the conspicuous absence of news from Chubut, made representations to the Argentine Government that a competent official should be delegated to ascertain how matters stood with the colony. Senor Tejidor, the Minister for Foreign Affairs, returned the somewhat non-commital reply that if it were in his power he would arrange such an inspection, but that months would elapse before a commission could be set on foot. (17) Whereupon MacDonnell, the Chargé d' Affaires pressed his own Government to approve the dispatch of a British naval vessel to Patagonia. The arrival of H.M.S. *Cracker* on April 4, 1871, was providential, for the settlers had been deliberating how to effect a permanent sealink with Buenos Aires, and what proposals should be submitted to the Argentine Government to reduce the dangers and effects of isolation. A free passage was offered to Lewis Jones, the undisputed leader of the colony, as far as Montevideo. From there he was to proceed to Buenos Aires to put the case of the Welsh to the Government.

He found it almost impossible to do so. It was only through sheer obstinacy - he himself reckoned that he had visited Government House some 84 times before being granted a hearing, that Lewis Jones finally induced the authorities to grant money towards the purchase of a schooner to serve the settlement. The grant, however, was withdrawn as soon as it had been approved. The reason, Lewis Jones wrote to Mac-Donnell, was the Government's intention "to remove a people who have no wish to be removed, and who have already undergone the inconceivable privations of making a home in an uninhabited country." He repeated his complaint when he called on MacDonnell personally. The British Chargé d' Affaires listened sympathetically to his exposition of the needs of the colony but felt reluctant to intervene, "as I felt confident that the jealousy with which diplomatic interference in such matters is viewed by this Government might render his case hopeless." (18)

Nevertheless MacDonnell thought it incumbent upon him to take up the cudgels on behalf of the settlers. A meeting took place between him and Senor Tejidor, during which it became transparently clear that the paternalistic attitude of the Government, so noticeable in Rawson's days, had given place to a more calculating and harsher approach to the problem of the Welsh colony. Tejidor deprecated the idea that priority in Government assistance should be extended to Chubut when other regions needed similar encouragement, and were likely to prove more profitable to the Republic. What is more, Mac-Donnell sensed an undertone of resentment that he, as the representative of a foreign and interested power, should have entered a plea for the colonists. "I thought," so he informed the British Secretary for Foreign Affairs, "I could discern an after thought in his Excellency's mind that the support which Her Majesty's Government extended to this colony was not foreign to the arguments used when Congress rejected the original contract, viz: that wherever a body however small of the Anglo-Saxon race had established itself, it had always finally succeeded in possessing itself of the country, and that in this instance the colonists would be supported in their ambitious views by the neighbouring establishment of the Falkland Islands."

If Tejidor considered it opportune to refer to the persistence of certain anti-English sentiments in the Republic, MacDonnell, in his turn, assumed that it would be equally timely to draw the Minister's attention to other Argentine susceptibilities which were, perhaps, more dominant. He pointed out that Patagonia was disputed territory between the Argentine and Chile, that the maintenance of the Chubut colony at the trifling cost of a schooner of 80-90 tons would be useful to Buenos Aires in this connection, and that, "the doubts as to the sovereignty of the Argentine Government over that country might in some degree be dissipated if the Argentine Government were disposed to give Mr. Jones the post he seeks as their authority over the colony." He added, in a judicious attempt to remove any trace of premeditated collusion between him and the Chubut leader, that the British Government would regard this as the final and decisive opportunity for the colony to establish itself. Moreover, "Mr. Jones was willing on behalf of the colony to subscribe to any conditions to which the Government would wish to bind them in the future, if the Government would extend to them once more their support." Senor Tejidor looked thoughtful and promised to give the matter his full attention.

There is little doubt that MacDonnell's intercession considerably improved the prospects of obtaining the vessel which the colonists were convinced would provide the solution to all their problems. Before he left Buenos Aires for home in October that year, Lewis Jones assured him in a letter that "the colony is entirely indebted to your tact and perserverence for the possession of the vessel to be at its service." It was a genuine expression of gratitude but somewhat exaggerated, for in the meantime another exchange of opinions had taken place between MacDonnell and Senor Tejidor. This indeed revealed that the Argentine Government had readjusted its policy towards the Welsh settlers, but with an unmistakable political slant to it.

MacDonnell was told that the Welsh were to have their ship, but that they were expected to repay the 3000 silver dollars allotted by the authorities for its purchase. The condition was reasonable, but it was followed by a second which must have aroused apprehensions in the British Chargé d' Affaires. It was to the effect that Lewis Jones should employ his influence as head of the colony to induce his countrymen to accept Argentine citizenship. The conditions were to be incorporated in a petition signed by the Chubut leader and formally submitted to the Government. The document was eventually drawn up and Lewis Jones, as head of the community, undertook "to bring about that the members of which it is composed shall become Argentine citizens, compromising myself furthermore and from the present moment to request on the part of the Federal Judge the concession of citizenship of this country to myself." (19) On October 30, 1871, the Government nominated Lewis Jones as its representative or *Alcade* in Chubut with full responsibility for its civil administration.

The new schooner brought a cargo of provisions, clothing and implements, and the newly appointed *Alcade,* safely to Chubut. A short time after, however, the Government demanded its return for certain reasons, and the colony seemed fated to be condemned to isolation. But it is conceivable that some of its members may have realized that the imposition of an *Alcade,* even if he were a reputable Welshman, upon the colony was the thin edge of further governmental interference and supervision. What they may not have fully appreciated was that, a year or two before their landing on the Patagonian coast, a new Nationality Law had been passed by Congress categorically declaring that all persons born on Argentine territory were Argentine citizens irrespective of the nationality of their parents. (20) One of the provisions of the Law was that the sons of foreigners, including those of British stock, so born were liable to compulsory military service. It was a liability that was soon to impinge on the lives of the settlers and foment discord in Chubut.

If MacDonnell entertained any hope of being allowed to forget about Chubut for a little while, he soon relinquished it.

In January, 1872, a letter arrived from Michael D. Jones, and its contents aroused alarm and despondency in the conscientious Chargé d' Affaires. The sanguine Principal of Bala roundly criticised any scheme to remove the Welsh from Patagonia, and announced that hundreds of their compatriots in the United States were so exhilarated by the idea of an independent Welsh colony that they were preparing to leave for Chubut. (21)

The possible disastrous repercussions of such an influx of people upon a settlement barely able to maintain 150 colonists were evident to MacDonnell. He immediately protested to the Foreign Office in London that their impact on Chubut would be one of adding immeasurably to the problems of a community whose prospects of material development were jeopardized by insecurity of tenure and the insignificant value placed on their land. He was not reassured by Michael Jones's glowing description of the American emigrants as being of a superior class with adequate capital to revitalize the moribund economy of Chubut. He therefore suggested that " the Welsh people be disabused with regard to the prospect held out to them by certain parties who seem to have taken advantage of Captain Dennistoun's report to make it appear as if the settlement was prosperous and progressing." (22)

The Foreign Office weighed the advice of its Chargé d'Affaires and proceeded to do two things which lit a train of explosive reaction. It sent a copy of MacDonnell's despatch to Michael Jones, and proposed that any intending emigrant should be warned of the hardships he was likely to encounter in Patagonia. This it followed up by concurring with a request from the British Emigration Commission in London that an advertisement should appear in the form of a poster advising people to pause and reflect before venturing to Chubut.

There was an immediate counterblast from Bala. Michael Jones discounted MacDonnell's tale of woe, and enclosed copies of letters from the more responsible settlers in Patagonia. These spoke of steady if unspectacular progress particularly in pastoral farming, of the exploration of territory outside the settlement, and of the new impetus given to the cultivation of the soil by initial attempts at irrigation. A letter from Lewis Jones rebuffed any suggestion of abandoning the colony, and contained an eloquent appeal for more Welshmen to come to the support of their struggling but resolute country-men. "I am confident that the valley of the Chubut will never again be deserted, though it is left for ourselves to decide whether we or some other people will be the inhabitants . . . If Welsh emigrants do not come here soon, others will ere long." To this seemingly incontrovertible evidence of pulsating activity, Michael Jones added the comment that, "to stop emigration would be to damage the colony. What is needed is more emigrants with more capital and more labour to work the canal." He also stressed for good measure that a brig called the *Rush* had already left New York for the Argentine with a number of American Welsh on board, and that others were preparing to follow. Faced with this unequivocal declaration of faith in the future of the colony, and with the rather disconcerting fact that the Argentine Government itself was advertising for more settlers in reputable Welsh papers, the Foreign Office recommended that the British Emigration Commission should withdraw its cautionary poster.

It was, however, too late to avoid the outburst of indignation which its publication had aroused in the United States. Acting upon instructions from London, the British Consul in New York had taken all possible steps to cool the ardour of the American Welsh. The President of the St. David's Society and the ministerial fraternity in that city had been recruited to discourage emigration by depicting the destitution which reigned along the banks of the Chubut river. (23) The *Drych*, the Welsh newspaper with the widest circulation, dutifully printed official reports on the colony, and for the moment for-got its romantic interest in the supposed existence of Welsh speaking Indians to express its views on the veracity of the con-flicting rumours concerning Patagonia. It also invited its readers to ventilate their opinions, but urged them to do so in a spirit of sweet reasonableness. There was an instantaneous rumble of criticism which exploded into anti-English feelings, particularly from the direction of the American office of the Emigration and Commercial Patagonian Company at Youngstown in Ohio. The cardinal objective of this company, which had representatives throughout the United States, was to raise £50,000 in shares and use the money to promote emigration to Patagonia. It advocated quite openly the gradual transformation of the Chubut colony into a strong, independent and viable state. (24) It was not surprising therefore that it denounced both the British Emigration Commission's advertisement and the reports of British Government officials as deliberate fabrications, whose sole purpose was to stifle the Welsh emigration movement in the United States. In very forceful language the Company made it abundantly clear that the Welsh had no intention of remaining supinely recumbent in the coffin in which the English proposed to bury the nation, and were on the point of nailing it down. (25)

In other Welsh American circles the reaction was less clamant. There was general disapproval of any scheme to disband the Chubut settlement, but it was recognized that to ignore certain real problems would be to invite disaster. In the circumstances this was a correct appraisal of the prospects facing emigrants, even those possessing capital. However, few of the American Welsh who had embarked so enthusiastically on the *Rush* reached Chubut. The majority, daunted by the hardships of the voyage, left the ship at Montevideo, an act of renunciation which had the effect of producing one of the first literary compositions of the Chubut colony in the form of a satirical poem entitled "The Emigrants who turned back."

The chagrin of the Chubut settlers was understandable since the successful implementation of a new scheme of irrigation, which required an extensive system of canals, depended upon an adequate supply of labour, and this could only be provided by fresh emigrants. But they overrated the capacity of the colony to absorb them and when, between September 1875 and January 1876 as many as 412 arrived from Wales, the settlement was overwhelmed by the demands made on its resources.

No preparations had been made for the reception of the new-comers; in fact, all surplus wheat had been transported for sale to Buenos Aires. The result was confusion, tension and considerable irritation among the newly arrived Welsh, who disliked the notion of having to live on the charity of the colonists or of the Argentine Government until the situation improved.

One proposal to relieve the burden was the ambitious one of establishing a second settlement on the south side of the river Santa Cruz, some 450 miles to the south of Chubut. Any objection from the Argentine Government could be discounted in advance, since a further practical step in the colonization of Patagonia would certainly not be taken amiss at a time when there was a substantial reduction in the flow of emigrants to the Argentine. (26) But before abandoning the comparative security of Chubut, the prospective pioneers were cautious enough to consult the British Government on the propriety of their plan, and the extent to which they could rely on British protection if they ran foul of other interested parties. Her Majesty's Government had no doubt where its duty lay. It agreed to exercise the minimal degree of intervention which it afforded to all British subjects resident in a foreign country. Beyond this it would not go, and in the case of Patagonia its prudence was fully justified. The proposed colony was to be set up on what was, politically speaking, combustible soil, and the risks were detectable to the Foreign Office which opined that, "it should be borne in mind that the territorial limits of Chile and the Argentine Government in Patagonia are still undecided, and the two Governments may come to blows about the question some day." (27)

The projected settlement did not materialize, and the reason was not only the noticeable lack of enthusiasm in London. Buenos Aires too had reached certain conclusions which were to have a profound effect on Chubut, and sensibly strengthen the control of the central government over the hitherto fortuitous development of the colony.

In one of his confidential communications to the Foreign

Office MacDonnell had predicted as far back as 1873 that, "should the colony become sufficiently strong and prosperous as to induce the Argentine Government to interfere in its administration (as it has reserved itself the right to do), the Chubut colonists must inevitably share the fate of the other frontier settlers in the Argentine Republic." (28)

The circumstances visualized by him were tangible enough in 1875-6 to convince the Argentine Government that it was time to integrate the colony in a national emigration scheme, and subordinate it to a more uniform structure of colonial administration and expansion. The authorities now considered it highly invidious that the Welsh should conduct their affairs haphazardly, when it was estimated that fifteen million immigrants were needed to develop the Republic whose population numbered little more than one and three quarter millions. Moreover, in Chubut itself, the dramatic proliferation of a static community into a colony of 700 people almost overnight presented difficulties which no amount of local ingenuity or resilience could resolve. It entailed, for instance, the further and equitable distribution of land, more extensive irrigation and better trading facilities, if the colony was to prosper and the Republic benefit from its progress. These were matters which could only be effectively dealt with by direct Government action.

The first step made by the Argentine Government was to pass a special law providing for the survey and delimitation of all the territory from the mouth of the Chubut river to the foothills of the Andes some three hundred miles to the west. It was proposed to operate the law as a pilot plan before proceeding to formulate a more general and comprehensive Land and Colonial Project for the Republic. At the same time surveyors were dispatched to Chubut to determine the allocation of land, and a Commissary nominated by the Government to be its official representative in the colony.

The appointment did not please the settlement which had been self-governing for the past ten years. Senor Onito was not an Argentine citizen by birth, neither were his duties sufficiently defined to reassure the Welsh as to the degree of his authority over their affairs. The tardiness and arrogance of the surveyors did not endear them to the settlers, and the failure of the Government to issue its long promised title deeds to the original emigrants provoked further discontent. Nevertheless, the situation showed definite signs of improvement. A new expedition was organized to explore the interior, supplies from Buenos Aires ensured ample food stocks, and in 1876 the colony was able to boast that its exports of wheat, butter, seal-skins - for some of the Welsh had taken to seal hunting, and other commodities had reached the respectable total of £7000. The colony could now relax enough to hold annual Eisteddfodau, and regard its initial miseries and privations as things of the past by celebrating its "Gwyl y Glaniad" (the first landing of the emigrants on July 28, 1865) with concerts, races and other pleasant distractions. (29)

Not that everything was idyllic, of course. Alarums and moments of anxiety still persisted. A few starving and ragged convicts did actually cross into Patagonia under the impression that they would be welcome, and were immediately clapped into prison. (30)

Another quiver of apprehension was felt when, in October 1878, Congress recommended that an offensive should be launched to expel the Indians from the territory which they had occupied, and extend the frontiers of the province of Buenos Aires to the Rio Negro. The introduction of the Remington quick-firing rifle disposed of the natives, but the danger of a retaliatory attack by the defeated tribes on the defenceless Welsh colony was very much alive to Ford, the British Minister in Buenos Aires. He drew the attention of the authorities to the "painful impression that would be caused in England were any disaster to befall it." (31) There was a soothing official disclaimer that the extermination of the Indians might adventitiously involve that of the Welsh. It was given by General Roca, then Minister of War, who was shortly to be elected President of the Republic, and who would show a greater tenacity than Senor Rawson in bringing Patagonia within the fold of the Argentine Confederation.

Possessing tremendous qualities of leadership and uninhibited visions of Argentine political and economic predominance, Roca was persuaded that success was conditional upon the stability of internal order, the expansion of railways to ensure an efficient network of communications, the definitive elimination of Indian incursions by the thorough subjugation of the tribes, and the unchallenged exercise of government authority and jurisdiction over every inch of national territory. Once these conditions had been achieved, he believed that the future of regions like Patagonia would be assured. "Let us offer," he declared, "a solid guarantee for their lives and property to those who bring their capital and their brawny arms to the work of fertilizing these regions, and we shall soon see multitudes of men of all countries and races pour into them, and new states arise to the greater power and greatness of the Republic." (32)

The potentially damaging effects of President Roca's colonization policy on the strictly Welsh character of the Chubut settlement were apparent to very few of the colonists at the time. The majority were primarily concerned with the dilatoriness of the Government in granting them the title deeds of their lands, and with the ineptitude of the Argentine officials closer at hand. It was now that an unexpected development occurred in the hitherto distant relations between the colony and the British Government, when it was proposed that a Vice-Consul should be appointed to solemnize marriages amongst the settlers and to act in an advisory capacity. The new British Minister at Buenos Aires, Sir Horace Rumbold, was consulted on the propriety of entrusting the office to Lewis Jones, and his reply hinted at certain complications unknown, perhaps, to London. "The present position of the settlers ... would appear to be a somewhat anomalous one inasmuch as they seem indisposed to become subjects of the country in which they have settled. It may, perhaps, be doubted whether such a state of things will be tolerated much longer by the Argentine Government." (33)

Rumbold did not elaborate on the situation, but one fact was

fairly evident. Lewis Jones's undertaking to persuade his
fellow colonists to apply for Argentine citizenship had
remained largely inoperative. However, the British Minister
welcomed the suggestion that he should be nominated unpaid
Vice-Consul at Chubut. To his surprise it was Lewis Jones
himself who rejected the idea, and the reason emerged during
an interview between the two men. "The object in view in
making such an appointment, namely the better protection of
the British subjects residing there, would be equally well
obtained if he, Mr Jones, were to be named instead by the
Argentine Government to the post of their National
Emigration Commissioner at Chubut. In this way the absurd
but - as Mr Jones assured me - very real fear of British
interference in the colony would be allayed, and the fussy and
vexatious conduct of the petty Argentine officials, such as the
Captain of the Port and its Inspector of Customs, efficiently
checked." (34)

Rumbold dismissed as nonsensical the notion that a Vice-
Consulship at Chubut could be possibly regarded as British
interference when, in fact, it served to confirm Argentine
authority over Patagonia. But he was prepared to advise the
Foreign Office to drop the whole idea, if Lewis Jones obtained
the Commissionership. The following day, the Chubut leader
was able to inform him that he had been appointed to the post
with a salary of £300 a year.

Whether Lewis Jones acted judiciously in this matter may
appear debatable in the light of subsequent events. The
proposal for British consular representation at Chubut had
been put forward in London after a careful consideration of a
report from Captain Erskine of H.M.S. *Garnet,* who had spent
some days in the colony in April, 1880. The difficulties con-
fronting the community had been eased by exceptionally good
harvests, and the eight hundred settlers were genuinely
appreciative of the generous treatment which they had received
at the hands of the Argentine Government. But Captain
Erskine discerned an embryonic conflict of wills between the
Welshmen and the Argentine officials, who, he wrote, "have at

least been unfortunate in their endeavours to uphold the dignity of their Government, and they have certainly not succeeded in winning either the respect or affection of the colonists." (35)

A number of factors, besides the perennial complaint of the non-materialization of title deeds, had contributed to this state of affairs. For the first time, the colonists were called upon to pay taxes and customs dues, which amounted to 40% on all exports. There was also some arbitrary interference with local industries, especially seal hunting. But there were two issues that vitally affected the domestic life of the colony, and on these there was an irreconcilable divergence of opinion.

The first concerned the solemnization of marriages which were performed in the local chapels according to Protestant rites. Since the Argentine Government was reluctant to concede their validity, there was naturally deep concern that they would not be recognized in the eyes of the law, whether Argentine or English. The appointment of a British consul with authority to solemnize marriages would have removed such fears. Failing this, the problem contained the germs of a bitter religious dispute between the settlers and the authorities.

The second issue, which promised a more intransigent attitude on the part of the Welsh, was the advertised intention of the Argentine Government to introduce a garrison at Chubut. It was a distasteful prospect for the colonists who shared the conviction of all classes in the Republic that the army consisted of the most disreputable elements in the land, and feared that their presence would lead to crime where there had been none hitherto, and alienate the friendly Indians in the vicinity. There were rumours that there would be a general exodus of settlers if soldiers were brought to Chubut. What is more pertinent, the very notion of having a garrison in their midst stiffened the resolution of the Welsh not to become naturalized Argentinians.

Viewing the inevitable conflict that was inherent in the situation, Captain Erskine had concluded in his report that the question of political status was likely to replace that of economic success or failure with the passage of time, and to him, at least, the position was clear. "The colony has undoubtedly the germs of British law-abiding propensities, and it is important that it should not be allowed to degenerate under the baneful influences of loose government."

The Boundaries Treaty between Chile and the Argentine ratified by Congress on October 22, 1881, removed the territorial bone of contention between the two countries by recognizing Argentine sovereignty over Patagonia from the Rio Negro to Terra del Fuego. It was also the signal for a more methodical application of President Roca's plan to convert the vast province into a region of prosperous settlements by generous land concessions, and where the Government's authority would encounter no local opposition or insubordination.

The imposition of economic control and provincial administration could not be achieved without eliminating resistance wherever the Argentine Government thought it existed. The Indian population was the first object of attention, and the policy adopted was one of virtual extermination. Except in one or two quarters it met with little criticism. The Bishop of the Falkland Islands, deploring the adamant attitude of the Government, expressed his opinion bluntly in the statement that, "the white man wants the land and the native of the soil must die." (36) There is evidence that many English and European settlers shared the conviction of official circles, and of public opinion generally, that the physical liquidation of the Indians could be condoned in the interests of civilisation and material progress.

It was an argument thoroughly repugnant to the Welsh at Chubut. From the first days of the colony they had entertained the friendliest feelings for the natives, who had played no small part in the survival of the original settlers. This harmonious coexistence had led to close trading relations, and before the Argentine soldiers swept them from the land, more than 1500 Indians were peaceably engaged in a mutually profitable system of barter and exchange which accounted for half the value of the total produce of Chubut. It was significant that the non-racialist behaviour of the Welsh was resented by the Argentine Government and public. "There is no doubt that the success of the Welshmen in establishing friendly commercial relations with the neighbouring Indian tribes, effected by the pursuance of a policy of humanity and honest dealing, had been resented by the Argentinians. . . . The example afforded by the Welsh colony of the possibility of humanising them (the Indians) by fair treatment has only aroused the jealousy and vindictiveness of those who preach and practise the sanguinary doctrine of wholesale indiscriminate massacre." (37)

Monson, the British Minister at Buenos Aires, who unreservedly expressed his high esteem of the Welsh in these words, was as anxious as his predecessor, Ford, had been, that their orderly progress and particular way of life should not be jeopardized by the repressive policy of the Government. He was not thinking, however, in terms of retaliatory raids and depredations by the surviving elements of the decimated tribes, but of more far-reaching consequences. "I am not without apprehension," he confessed in the same despatch to the Foreign Office, "that under these altered circumstances there will be less inclination on the part of the Government to recognise or satisfy the claims of the Welshmen to any moderate species of self-government."

Monson was fully justified in his fears. For some time the modest system of independent local administration set up by the colonists had been steadily breached, and finally dismantled by government pressure. The first move in this direction had been the dismissal of Lewis Jones from his post as Commissary barely six months after his appointment. He had been replaced by an Argentine Commissary who habitually spent four months every year in Buenos Aires, and whose absence meant that there was no official in Chubut invested with sufficient power to attend to the legal and administrative exigencies of a colony which now numbered more than 1400 people. Friction between them and the new

Commissary was unavoidable, and resulted in open confrontation when Lewis Jones refused to provide personal data for the Commissary's annual report, on the grounds that the method of collecting statistics about the colony was suspect. He was placed under arrest, and when his countrymen gathered together in a chapel to discuss his predicament, they were charged with holding a riotous assembly. The Chubut leader was taken to Buenos Aires, and underwent the humiliating experience of being detained in an insalubrious cell reserved for political prisoners before being released after three months of involuntary exile in the capital.

The incident served to bring into prominence what had increasingly become a quarrel between the colony and the Government over the question of local liberties. Briefly, the Welsh claimed certain municipal rights, such as the election of a local council and Justice of the Peace, which they charged the Government with flagrantly denying to them in direct contravention of the law of the land. The particular law which they had in mind was the Colonization Law of 1876, which provided for municipal institutions in colonies established on national territories, the latter, of course, comprising Patagonia. Article 119 of the Law stipulated that as soon as fifty families had been settled in any such colony, they would be empowered to choose their municipal authorities. The Chubut colony had long since complied with the statistical requirements of the law, but had not been granted the prescriptive electoral rights. The grievances of the Welsh stemmed therefore from the indisputable fact that, despite the Colonization Law, they were deprived of their statutory right to a measure of control over their own affairs. Moreover, they had no means of representation, no unprejudiced access to the Government, not even the minimum right to be consulted on matters concerning the everyday life of the community. All military and political power was exercised by the Commissary, but the limits of his authority were so vague that he could trespass on the civic liberties which the Colonization Law recognized as pertaining to the colonists.

What aggravated the situation still further was the fundamental difference of approach of the Welsh settlers and the
Argentine Government towards the concept of local government. To the former a democratic procedure of election, such
as they had formerly employed in choosing their council, was
indispensable in the interests of justice, integrity and efficiency.
As former British citizens they could envisage no other. But in
the form advocated and practised by them it was a challenge to
the centralist doctrines of the Republic, which dictated that all
subordinate officials should be nominated by the Government, and be entirely responsible to the latter, and not to the
community. This was partly a legacy of the former Spanish
colonial administration, but recent political disturbances had
shown the dangers of a divided authority within the Republic.
A protracted struggle with certain provincial governments, of
which there were as many as fourteen, marked by periodic
insurrections and the threat of secession by some regional
governors, had made the central Government very much aware
of the inadvisability of delegating too much local autonomy to
distant regions. Isolated from the theatre of these domestic
conflicts, the Chubut settlers had had little occasion to
appreciate the circumstances which impelled the Argentine
Government to institute a rigorous supervision over regional
jurisdiction and administration, with little or no regard for
local feeling.

Monson had foreseen where these developments were likely
to lead in Patagonia. "It can, I think, hardly be expected that
the Argentine Government will tolerate pretensions to
exclusiveness and self-government which, in the originally
isolated condition of the Colony and even in its present comparative remoteness, the Welshmen are not to be blamed for
formulating." (38) At the same time he put his finger on the
prime cause of any future contention between the colonists and
the Government. It lay in the ignorance of the Welsh who are
too inclined to assume that, "the police and general administrative system in force in the provinces of this Republic
resemble the municipal institutions of Great Britain." (39)

In view of the smouldering resentment in Chubut, Monson thought it expedient to bring the complaints of the colonists to the attention of the Argentine Government. In a *note verbale* he suggested that the reinstatement of Lewis Jones as Commissary would go a long way towards conciliating the Welsh. The proposal was rejected, and when Monson reminded the Government that London was interested in the treatment and welfare of the colonists, Ortez, the Argentine Minister for Foreign Relations, rejoined bluntly, "that a colony of foreigners arriving in a country enjoying its own independent rights could [not] have any pretext for expecting that they would be allowed to introduce their own municipal institutions and ignore the authority and even the language of the national Government." (40) But he added that Congress was considering legislation whereby Justices of the Peace would be appointed by the Government to districts like Chubut to take cognizance of minor civil and criminal affairs, exercise the functions of chief of police, and preside over municipal bodies when and where these would be organized with the active participation of the inhabitants of those districts.

These measures, although constructive, were far removed from the Colonization Law of 1876, which had stipulated that Justices of the Peace and municipal bodies should be elected locally. But the all-important Clause 119 that embodied that concession also contained the provision that their functions should be determined by the Executive power until specific laws defining them had been passed. It was precisely the interpretation of this clause that exacerbated feelings on both sides. The Chubut Welsh claimed that it should be implemented without any reservation whatsoever. On the other hand, Dr. Iriqoyen, the Argentine Minister of the Interior, insisted that further laws were necessary to formulate in precise terms the authority of both Justices of the Peace and municipal corporations before they could be properly established. For his part, Monson was inclined to believe that the conditional provision in the clause still enabled the Government to delay granting to the Welsh what they thought them-selves legally entitled to. "It certainly would seem to be an un-fair interpretation of the law to say that, as the Central Govern-ment has the right to define the functions of the Justice of the Peace and Municipals, it is justified in defining them as non-existent." (41) Lewis Jones's feelings and language were less restrained. "The Government undoubtedly aims at crushing our Britishism and making gauchos of us. We are what the London *World* called "splendidly stubborn" on the point and will struggle on, come what may." (42)

Little more could be done, for a further note addressed by Monson inquiring why the Colonization Law should remain inoperative in Chubut was virtually ignored by the Government. In the following year the issue was permanently settled by the Government, which took the step of in-corporating the colony into a district and appointing a Governor to reside officially in Rawson. It thereby irrevocably dismissed the possibility that Chubut would ever enjoy any autonomous political or administrative status, and made it clear that the Welsh were henceforth immutably attached to the laws and customs of the Republic.

The integration of the colony in the body politic of the Argentine might have been expected to produce some re-action, but it would appear that the sense of civic injustice which had permeated the community was dispelled by a mood of optimism. This may have been partly due to the appoint-ment of Luis Fontane as the first Governor. An enlightened and considerate administrator, he won the confidence of the settlers by allowing them to settle their disputes through arbitrators of their own choice, and by refraining from opposition to measures devised by them in the general interest of the colony. A further factor which helped to create a better atmosphere was the belated grant of title deeds to about half the 335 farmers in the Chubut valley.

Even so, there was still an abundance of smouldering grievances which could be fanned at any time into hotbeds of dissension. It was felt, for instance, that the Government was particularly remiss in not subsidizing irrigation projects with which the colonists had to cope single-handed. A decree of November, 1884, which committed the authorities to provide the necessary equipment for the construction of dams, but only on the condition that the settlers were prepared to work gratuitously on the sites, was shrugged off as unacceptable. To the Welsh the Government seemed to be more concerned with building schools, in which the pupils were monoglot Welsh children and the language of instruction exclusively Spanish. No one disputed that a knowledge of Spanish was highly desirable, but there was an uneasy feeling abroad that the purpose of such schools was the political one of enforcing linguistic uniformity as a preliminary step towards the eventual denationalization of the Welsh. Moreover, the absence of a medical service was attributed to the negligence or indifference of the Government. There had been no resident doctor in the colony since the early months of 1866, and the community had relied on the medical staff of visiting British warships for pharmaceutical supplies and surgical treatment. The health of the settlers hitherto had been astonishingly good, but with the increase in population existing sanitary arrangements were insufficient and could become harmful.

For the moment, however, the consensus of opinion in Chubut allowed that these were grievances which could be adjusted in time. The prospects for the colony were heartening enough in 1885 for its leaders to contemplate one or two ambitious schemes. For instance, Lewis Jones drew up a plan for the construction of a railway to link Chubut with Port Madryn, which would cheapen as well as expedite the transport of the produce of the valley to that port, and its shipment on board chartered sloops plying between it and Buenos Aires. The Government willingly granted a railway concession, and the successful formation of a company in England with a capital of £60,000 provided the necessary financial impetus for the work to begin in 1886. By May, 1887, it was in full swing, and a pier had been built at Port Madryn as a complimentary part of the scheme.

Unfortunately, the hopes of its promoters were to evaporate like a chance shower of rain on the parched land of Chubut. The track pushed forward rapidly but its costs grew with each mile. Workers and engineers were brought over from Britain, some four hundred of them, and their expectations of good pay and food proved as shortlived as the financial anticipations of their employers. Once again in the history of Chubut a project was launched without a preliminary and cautious exploration of what was attainable in that land. Since passenger traffic would be at a minimum amongst a people who rarely left their homes unless it were never to return, the operations of the railway would be confined to the movement of the principal crop, which was wheat. But eight thousand tons of that cereal was the highest conceivable output in Chubut, where only one-fifth of the land was under cultivation, and any vagaries of weather could curtail that amount drastically. With an average load of one hundred tons, even the most sanguine investor in the Chubut Company had to admit that eighty train journeys a year would suffice to convey all available stocks of wheat to Port Madryn. (43)

It was enough to debilitate the most modest hope of extracting a dividend. But acting on the assumption that the colony would be forced to use the railway, with its offer of a regular service providing an outlet to the expanding grain market in Buenos Aires, the Company imposed the onerous freight charge of £1 for the 45 mile journey to Port Madryn. Compared with the normal charge of 15/9 for the lengthy sea voyage from Port Madryn to Liverpool, this was almost prohibitive. The first reaction of the colonists was one of indignation, and there was some heated talk of transporting the grain down the river in small boats to Port Madryn where some ocean-going vessel would pick it up and carry it to the Argentine capital. Any competitive scheme of this kind was sheer hallucination, as the hard-pressed settlers knew too well, and they resigned themselves with an ill grace to the demands of the Company. The mood of the colonists never changed; on one occasion they even rejected an offer by the Company to assist in repairing certain damage done to irrigation works. Such was the regrettable lack of harmony between them that as late as 1891 the Company was obliged to reduce its services to one train a week. The more incorrigible of the colonists may have been pleased with this inactivity. What they did not appreciate was the fact that it was used as an argument by the British Government against establishing a Vice-Consular post in Chubut when that question was enthusiastically revived by the community in the same year, and was rather summarily dismissed by Lord Salisbury, the Secretary for Foreign Affairs.

In another direction the Welsh showed greater determination and flexibility. After twenty years or so of comparative immobility, the feeling grew amongst them that the colony required an outlet, not only for its wheat, but for some of its inhabitants as well. The valley had become too small to accommodate a population that had increased, in spasmodic bursts, from eight hundred in 1880 to two thousand in 1889. The problem of finding land for new immigrants had been complicated by the action of the Argentine Government. With an eye on the mounting value of land, it had taken possession of unoccupied territory in Chubut, and made a practice of granting portions of it to local officials. The result was that speculation had become rife, and the possibility of obtaining plots, except by buying or renting them at excessive rates, correspondingly restricted. The natural predisposition of the Welsh, like other colonists, to expend their energy in cultivating land which they could call their own, and not in the interests of other people, forced them to cast about for virgin territory. They found it at the foot of the Andes some four hundred miles to the west. Under the enterprising leadership of T. M. Thomas, popularly known as the Stanley of Patagonia, an expedition left the valley in 1888 and penetrated the little known hinterland between Chubut and the Cordilleras. On October 16, after an exhausting journey they discovered an ideal site for a settlement and, inspired by the magnificent view, called it Cwm Hyfryd. The news was received with exultation in Chubut. Governor Fontane himself visited the locality and recommended immediate occupation and development. The rumour that gold had been found there naturally roused excitement, and was to feed the hopes of prospectors for many years. Even Lewis Jones, who was not given to exaggeration, expressed a fear that the colony might well witness a gold rush which would infect the essentially Welsh character of the community. But he must have instinctively felt that the real danger did not emanate from that quarter.

The problem that undoubtedly weighed heavily on the mind of Lewis Jones and other leaders was how to preserve the homogeneity of the Chubut colony. So far the community was almost entirely Welsh in language and sentiment. In 1890 there were 2500 Welshmen as opposed to about one hundred Argentine officials. Four years later the population had grown to 3000, but this number included other foreigners, mostly Italians, and the proportion of the non-Welsh element showed every sign of increasing in the future. The fact that the colony was now divided into two municipalities, Rawson and Gaiman, opened the way to a multiplicity of Government appointed officials, of whom there were already more than enough in the opinion of the colonists. But there were two other factors militating against the preservation of the distinctively Welsh character of the Chubut colony.

One was the falling off in the intermittent arrival of immigrants from Wales, consequent upon the warning of the British Government that prospective settlers would do well to avoid the Argentine and proceed to Canada, Australia and South Africa. Poor reception facilities, armed internal revolts, political confusion and, above all, financial crises were all adduced as good reasons for not venturing to the Argentine. (44) They would appear to have had a restraining effect in Britain. The second factor was a change in the attitude of the Argentine Government towards one important aspect of its immigration policy. After decades of unrestricted entry, it had suddenly realized that the new settlers were preponderantly South European, and that the predominance of one people or another, particularly if concentrated within certain areas,

could prove deleterious to national unity. The rumours of a
projected insurrection by the Italian section of the inhabitants
of Buenos Aires had already spelt out the dangers of such a
situation. A more even distribution and judicious mixture of
immigrants was therefore thought desirable, not least in the
outlying provinces of the Republic, where clashes between
well-organized foreign communities and Argentine adminis-
trators were frequent and sometimes violent.

One way of circumventing a disproportionate influx of other
foreigners into Chubut, or so it seemed to the Welsh, was the
obvious one of planting offshoots of the colony wherever
possible, and so bringing as much of the region as they could
under Welsh influence. As far back as 1880 one of Lewis
Jones's closest collaborators. R. J. Berwyn, had foreseen the
consequences of neglecting to do so, but any extension of the
colony's frontiers required a constant stream of Welsh
immigrants to provide the necessary man power and capital.
Without them schemes of settlement, however enterprising,
were doomed to failure. The expedition to the Andes, it is true,
was a success and a resounding one at that. But two other
attempts to found small colonies, one to the south of Chubut
between the coast and Lake Colwapi, the other 120 miles to the
west of Rawson, had to be abandoned owing to the lack of
settlers.

These and other considerations may have prevailed upon the
colony to reopen the question of appointing an unpaid British
Vice-Consul at Chubut. On this occasion Lewis Jones
associated himself unreservedly with a memorial on the subject
addressed to Lord Salisbury, the Secretary for Foreign Affairs,
in August 1889, and signed by twenty two prominent members
of the community. It stressed that growing trade relations with
the outside world, the complexities of commercial and land
transactions, the comparative inaccessibility of British
consular officials in Buenos Aires, and. not least, the movement towards the plantation of new settlements in Patagonia,
were all developments that required the presence of a Vice-
Consul in Rawson. The memorial also recommended that the

post should be given to Llwyd ap Iwan, one of the two sons of Michael D. Jones who had settled in Chubut, and whose future role in the colony's history was to be one of significance. He was, the memorial stressed, "a man of good abilities, of an honourable disposition and of exemplifying habits," who enjoyed the additional qualification of having been educated as a civil engineer in London and Germany. (46)

Despite the fact that nine years previously it had itself initiated a similar proposal, the British Government displayed little interest in the arguments put forward in the memorial. It was reluctant to believe that British interests in Chubut were important enough to justify such an appointment, and, reversing roles with Lewis Jones, it was inclined to think that the appearance of a British Vice-Consul on the scene might lead to friction with the Argentine officials. In a further communication some time later, Lewis Jones suggested that if a salary were attached to the post,the Argentine Government would be disarmed of all suspicions and regard it as a simple commercial appointment primarily concerned with shipping and ancillary matters. He added that he was prepared to be considered for the post, an offer which drew the rather uncomplimentary comment from London that the Foreign Office doubted whether "the Vice-Consulship is required as much for British shipping as for Mr. Jones." (47) It was an attitude which ignored the genuine apprehensions and wishes of the colonists. It proved impervious even to the intervention of T.E.Ellis, the influential member for Merioneth and Government Whip, who wrote personally to Edward Grey that Lewis Jones was eminently qualified to act as Vice-Consul.

There was little the Welsh could do except hope that events would induce the Foreign Office to change its mind. In the meantime they could comfort themselves with the fact that materially the colony was in fairly good shape. The introduction of alfalfa gave a fillip to an economy which was too dependent upon wheat growing, and there was a visible improvement in housing and social amenities. Curiously enough, there was no corresponding invigoration of the more cultural expressions of Welsh life. The *Drafod* edited by Lewis Jones, and the sole purveyor of local and foreign news in the vernacular, suspended publication for some time. And a school opened by his niece and his daughter to provide higher education for Welsh girls was forced to close down for want of support. But these discouraging developments were overshadowed in 1895 by the recall of Governor Fontane, who for ten years had identified himself with the progressive activities of the colonists and enjoyed the confidence of the whole community. His departure was viewed with despondency and a general feeling that his successor might be a person of less charitable disposition and understanding. Predictions of disagreement and tension again filled the air. "I am certain," wrote a visiting English naval commander, "the colonists do not admire the Argentine officials . . . although the late Governor was a capital man and did a great deal for them, but from my experience I should think he was an exceptional man." (48)

The recall of Senor Fontane did, in fact, abruptly terminate all amicable collaboration between colonists and officials. During the ensuing years his successors managed to convert the Welsh into a sullen and resentful community. Senor Tello, who replaced him, made his attitude unmistakably clear by issuing three decrees which were bound to exasperate the colonists. One ordered that all youths over eighteen, born in Chubut, should enrol in the National Guard commanded by Argentine officers. Another declared Sunday to be the appointed day for drilling, and punished non-compliance with imprisonment. A third decree proclaimed the right of the Government to interfere with the management of the canals which had been constructed entirely through the physical exertions of the Welsh. It was argued that Congress or the executive power were entitled to regulate their use on the grounds that the irrigation channels, although private property, were supplied with water from the River Chubut which was Government owned.

Delegations and protests were not completely ignored in

Buenos Aires where the Government, after some deliberation, agreed that drilling should be held on a weekday instead of Sunday. But the situation deteriorated when Colonel O'Donnell took over the reins of Governorship. He chose to discount the decision of the Government and to flout the religious susceptibilities of the settlers. Claiming to be the sole competent authority in Chubut he insisted on Sunday parades and openly declared, for good measure, that the community would do well to remember that the Chubut existed for the Argentine people and not for the Welsh. Later, he followed this up with a request to Buenos Aires for the stationing of a garrison in Chubut, which was granted to the consternation of the pacifist Welsh. But it is possible that the worst fears of the latter were roused by the report of the Governor which was printed in *La Nacion* on December 9, 1898, when he inveighed against the Welsh schools in the valley and demanded the substitution of Argentine masters for those who instructed the pupils in Welsh language and culture. To the leaders of the colony the Governor's policy pointed to a deliberate campaign for the eventual elimination of every vestige of Welsh nationality and tradition. It was even feared by some of them that with the troops at his disposal, O'Donnell might be tempted to embark on forcible denationalization.

In fact they had already decided to throw down the gauntlet and challenge the Governor to subvert the traditional way of life, which they had laboriously tried to preserve over the years. And there was a touch of militancy in their proceedings which was unprecedented, and showed that they had reached the limits of their endurance under the constant provocations of the Argentine officials. On September 5, 1898, a secret meeting of the heads of the most reputable families was convened in the chapel at Gaiman. There, behind locked doors, the whole position was reviewed, the absolute incompatability of the attitudes of Governor O'Donnell and the colonists confirmed, and certain resolutions taken. The most far-reaching and uncompromising of these was the decision to send two delegates to London. They were authorized, in the name of the colony, to seek an interview with the Foreign Office, and to submit a memorial which not only arraigned the Governor but contained an appeal for the direct intervention of the British Government. The mission was entrusted to Llwyd ap Iwan and T. Benbow Phillips, and without further delay they made their way to Buenos Aires to board a ship for England.

The Chubut delegates arrived in London early in 1899, and on February 28 they submitted a signed statement to the Foreign Office. It was a trenchant criticism of Argentine administration within the colony during the past four years, and ended on a particularly vitriolic note. Castigating the proposal to bring Argentine troops to Chubut, which appeared dangerous as well as offensive to the Welsh, the memorial declared that, "life and property will not be safe, and the honour of women will be at the mercy of a licentious half-caste soldiery composed of assassins and the sweepings of the jails. The Welsh, whether they wish it or not, will be driven into making reprisals and Chupat will then become an Argentinian Cuba."

The means of redress suggested by the memorial were extreme enough to bring any British Foreign Secretary to his feet in surprise and alarm. It called for a bold and sweeping action - nothing less than a formal proclamation by the British Government that Patagonia was British territory. History, the two delegates maintained, would substantiate the claim. In 1670, Sir John Narborough had landed on the coast of Patagonia, hoisted the British flag and taken possession of the land in the name of King Charles II. Up to 1865 no other nation had asserted any legal right to it in accordance with international law. The colonization of Chubut in that year not only revived but rendered permanent the sovereignty of Britain over Patagonia. If by chance the Monroe Doctrine were to cast a shadow over the indisputable rights of Britain, then, the statement went on, her Majesty's Government might choose to act in concert with the American Government - there being a number of American Welsh in Chubut - and designate Patagonia, or at least the Chubut valley, as an independent state under the protection of Britain and the United States. (49)

The feelings of Lord Salisbury, the Foreign Secretary, upon perusing this explosive document, can be surmised. He had long held the view that colonies were undesirable, both on the grounds of expense and the ever present danger that they might involve Britain in foreign disputes. (50) To him the recognition of existing frontiers by all countries was a positive obligation if territorial conflicts were to be avoided. To ward off the ultimate evil of war had been the cardinal aim of his policy on the two occasions he held the office of Foreign Secretary. Undoubtedly the grievances of the Welsh excited his sympathy, but the territorial solution propounded by them must have appeared to him irresponsible in the highest degree. It would also be politically dangerous if it were ever to commend itself to a section of the British public, as could very well happen in a country where the expression of opinion was uninhibited. However, he decided to consult legal and diplomatic experts before committing himself to an official reply.

While Llwyd ap Iwan and Benbow Phillips were drawing up their memorial in London, President Roca had suddenly appeared in Chubut. "His Excellency," wrote Barrington, the British Minister, to London, "paid a visit to Chubut and to the Welsh Colony there, by whose members he appears to have been well received, and towards whom, I am assured, he is well disposed, such colonists being of the class whom he would like to see settling in the wide southern territories now practically unoccupied. He ascribes no importance to the scheme set on foot by two members of the Welsh community in question who recently went to England with the view of trying to get a British protectorate established over the region laboriously opened up and managed by their countrymen, and the Minister for Foreign Affairs also gave no credit to the idea that her Majesty's Government seriously countenanced the suggested creation of an imperium in imperio." (51)

The President would seem to have made a commendable effort to conciliate Welsh opinion in Chubut. He listened carefully to the complaints submitted by the settlers, agreed that some were legitimate enough, and promised that they should receive fair consideration in Buenos Aires. For their part the colonists, or many of them, presented an address of welcome and hung out flags in his honour.

The President did not forget his obligations to the Welsh upon his return to the capital, although what followed brought as much apprehension as relief to them. Roca summoned a special meeting of his Cabinet on February 24 to discuss the affairs of Chubut. It was decided to abolish compulsory Sunday drill, establish an Agricultural School, and subsidize a line of steamers between Buenos Aires and Port Madryn. There could be no conceivable opposition to these constructive measures, but when the Cabinet went on to examine the problem of education certain prejudices were given a free rein. The Spanish language was to be made obligatory in the colony and Welsh discouraged by every means, even to the extent of replacing the present Welsh teachers by monoglot Argentine instructors. As to the inflammable divergence of opinion over military service, the youth of Chubut was not only to be made liable to conscription, but to be drafted out of the colony to Buenos Aires and elsewhere. In the place of the young Welshmen Argentine soldiers were to be stationed permanently in Chubut.

These latter resolutions ran counter to the wishes of the colonists with which Roca was fully conversant. They represented, in some measure, the sentiments of certain metropolitan newspapers which were conducting an anti-Welsh campaign at the time, and were not above advocating the summary ejection of the Welsh from Chubut. The British Minister in Buenos Aires was inclined to attribute this mood to the resentment created in Government circles and amongst the public by the secessionist proposals now being put forward in London by the two Chubut delegates. But if indignation in the capital confined itself to denunciations in the press, it took a dramatic form in the colony.

On January 29, 1899, within three days after the departure of President Roca, a detachment of police was sent by Governor O'Donnell to Trelew. It was a Sunday and the little chapel there was full of worshippers, amongst them the chairman and secretary of the committee, or the Colonial Council as it designated itself, which had dispatched Llwyd ap Iwan and Benbow Phillips to England. They received a peremptory summons to leave their devotions, and upon appearing outside they were arrested and conducted to Rawson. Here they were accused of high treason and placed in cells. Later the charges against them were disproved without difficulty, and they were unconditionally released. If this demonstration of *force majeure* was intended to cow men of the calibre of Lewis Jones, it failed in its purpose. But it was a forcible reminder that political action in the colony entailed risks for the protagonists of any ideas which the authorities considered to be subversive in any degree.

In the course of time the news of the arrests at Trelew reached Britain, and added an emotional undertone to the conflicting reactions produced by the memorial of the Chubut delegates to the Foreign Office.

The Argentine Ambassador wished Lord Salisbury to understand that the opinions expressed in it represented, in no way, those of the colonists in general. On the contrary they were content to be in the Republic, and had shown, during the visit of President Roca, that they were "good Argentine citizens." (52) The Liverpool *Mercury* begged to differ, and did so bluntly. In an article entitled "Strong Repressive Measures", the paper reviewed the situation at Chubut, and reserved its most excoriating comments for the decision of the Argentine Government to station troops in the colony. "There can be nothing in the state of the colony itself calling for this step, which is manifestly calculated to serve the double purpose of overawing the colonists and of emphasizing the Argentine decision to hold possession of the district against possible British (or American) intervention." (53) And from his retirement near Monmouth Vice-Admiral Brent, formerly in command of the British squadron in the south-east waters of America, fulminated against the subjection of industrious and idealistic Welshmen to what he termed a corrupt officialdom, and declared that "if her Majesty's Government can stand between the Welsh and the Argentine Government or become their protectors it would be a merciful and humane work. . . . I am wondering whether it would be possible to obtain the valley of the Chupat and the surrounding country as a Welsh Republic owing fealty to the Argentine Government." (54)

These were individual viewpoints which did not worry Lord Salisbury excessively. But what he could not ignore was the emergence of a pro-Chubut party amongst the Welsh Members of Parliament in the House of Commons, and their vociferous sympathy with the two representatives of the separatist movement amongst the colonists. The first indication of what was afoot came when a committee of Welsh members of all parties appointed three of their number - D. Brynmor Jones, Alfred Thomas and Tudor Howell (55) to request a meeting with Sir John Broderick, the Under-Secretary for Foreign Affairs, which was arranged for March 4th. At that meeting the three delegates, who were accompanied by Llwyd ap Iwan and Benbow Phillips, lost no time in elaborating two arguments. The first was to the effect that the Argentine Government exercised no valid sovereignty over Patagonia. If it did, so ran their second argument, then the colonists had an incontrovertible claim on the British Government to protect them as British subjects against the oppression of Argentine officials. After some discussion Broderick undertook to consider any legal points that could be advanced concerning the validity of Argentine sovereignty, and on this assurance the delegates withdrew. (56)

In a little over a month Broderick received a formal memorial from Brynmor Jones and his colleagues. It called for an inquiry by Lord Salisbury into all the circumstances of the case, and the adoption of one of two policies if the statements contained in the Chubut memorial were corroborated in substance. The first was to assert British sovereignty over the Chubut valley. If the Government felt disinclined to do this, it should request the Argentine Government to facilitate the re-

moval of those Welshmen who desired to emigrate to another
British colony, and compensate them adequately for their land
and stock. The alternative policy rested on the assumption that
the British Government would prefer to recognize Argentine
sovereignty over the whole of Patagonia. In this case, it was invited to press Buenos Aires for the enactment of special laws
protecting the Welsh against methods of government repugnant to their feelings, and ensuring that such laws were
expressly guaranteed by a treaty between the two countries.
(57)

One day sufficed for the legal experts in the Foreign Office to
demolish these forcible, but at the same time somewhat forced,
arguments. They made no bones that in their view Patagonia
was entirely Argentine territory. Not only had the first Welsh
emigrants acknowledged that fact by accepting both land and
assistance from the Argentine Government, but it was hardly
conceivable that they would have landed at Chubut in the first
place without the permission of Buenos Aires. To establish the
British character of Chubut, it would be necessary to prove
that the Queen of England had exercised acts of sovereignty
over it and treated the region as part and parcel of her
dominions, which was emphatically not the case. If the Crown,
for reasons of state, wished to assert a claim to Chubut as
British soil, it might do so by now adopting the various acts of
ownership, performed years ago by the colonists on their own
behalf, as having been done with the approval and connivance
of Queen and Government. This, however, would be "a little
too thin." In fact, "the colonists do not make out a rag of a
case." (58)

An answer along these lines was sent to Brynmor Jones on
May 3, and a few days later the British Minister in Buenos
Aires was informed that the Foreign Office would in no way
endorse the claim that, "the lands occupied by them (the
colonists) be recognised as British territory or an independent
state of Argentine under the joint Protectorate of Great Britain
and the Argentine Government." He was, however, to exert his
influence to protect the colonists against the vexations of
Argentine officials. (59)

In the hostile atmosphere of Buenos Aires the decision of his Government came as a relief to Barrington. But the directive to intervene on behalf of the Welsh, whenever he thought a de-marche justified, must have added to an already perplexing situation. Faced with a resuscitation of the old quarrel with Chile over frontiers, this time along the Andes, and with mounting disorder at home, the Argentine Government had re-solved on two draconian security measures. The one invested the Executive with summary powers to expel foreigners whose presence was considered incompatible with national interests. The other rendered liable to imprisonment any person who, with the connivance of a foreign Government, committed an act designed to bring national territory under foreign dominion. The authorities, as Barrington knew, were not acting without good reason. It was estimated that there were at least six thousand professed anarchists at large in the Republic, who had harboured and entertained the assassins of the Empress of Austria and the King of Italy. Later in the year they were to issue a manifesto declaring death to all European mon-archs, including Queen Victoria. Their activities and con-spiracies were certainly an obstacle to the growth of amicable relations between the Argentine and European Governments.

A study of these two stringent measures made Barrington somewhat uncomfortable, for the threat to the secessionists at Chubut was implicit in them. "Should these proposals," he commented in a despatch, "take the form of regular laws, especially the first of the two, I cannot but think that there may be the possibility of trouble in the future. However much it may be maintained that such a law could not be abused, it seems to me that its existence might open the door to proceedings of an arbitrary character against individuals who might have rend-ered themselves merely obnoxious in some way to the powers that be. The connection of both measures with what has recently been done by two members of the Welsh Colony in Chubut appears to be by no means excluded." (60)

But what Benbow Phillips and Llwyd ap Iwan had really done in London was to lay bare the resolution of the British

Government not to become identified with any disruptive action undertaken by the aggrieved colonists. This correctness of behaviour was further exemplified in the House of Commons on July 25, 1899, when Brynmor Jones, who still refused to be prised from his devotion to the Chubut Welsh, demanded whether the Government had received knowledge of the arrests in Trelew the previous January, and what it proposed to do to end such highhanded procedures. The Government's reply was scarcely reassuring, and was likely to be disturbing to British colonists other than those of Welsh blood within the Argentine. It stated that unless the two persons arrested on that occasion could prove that they had not been born on Argentine soil, they would be considered as Argentine citizens subject to the law and customs of the Republic. (61) There could have been no more unequivocal statement that henceforth the colonists would have to conform to Argentine administration, and could expect little more than benign mediation from the British Government in the matter of grievances as long as they remained resident on Argentine territory. It probably created much disappointment and, perhaps, a little bitterness in Chubut, but its apparent inflexibility brought the Welsh face to face with the realities of their situation. They could stay in the Argentine, if they so wished, and resign themselves to their lot in the hope that it might eventually improve. Alternatively, of course, they could emigrate.

The conflict of emotions aroused by the failure of the delegation in London was, however, submerged under the disaster which overwhelmed the colony in August, 1899. It had been raining abnormally during the early months of the year, an unprecedented five inches being registered up to the end of May. This had been a serious handicap to transport since there were no properly constructed roads in the valley, but the inconvenience was outweighed by the prospects of an abundance of water for future harvests. (62)

With little warning the River Chubut rose and inundated the valley. A mass of water tore its way through the irrigation canals and raced towards the sea, sweeping livestock and buildings before it. Rawson was almost obliterated, Gaiman extensively damaged, and scores of farms up and down the colony made uninhabitable. Some of the older settlers had to stand by helplessly and witness the ruination of the fruits of long years of unremitting labour. One of them was Lewis Jones, who found himself completely destitute at a time when he was incapacitated by illness. (63)

When the first shock was spent, the stubbornness of the early pioneering days reasserted itself. Help came quickly from Wales, and the Argentine Government immediately allocated £9000 towards the repair of the canals and farms. A great deal of reconstruction was achieved, but it was virtually impossible to eradicate the full effects of the disaster. Even after twelve months only 140 out of the 430 farms in the valley were capable of yielding more than a bare living for their owners, and the export of wheat from Chubut had dropped from 6000 to 1800 tons. (64) Even so, many of the colonists might have braced themselves to further efforts if the river had not drowned the valley for the second time in the following year.

It was now that the feeling spread that the whole purpose of the emigration to Patagonia was visionary and impractical. It was not only physical tribulations that produced this sense of disillusionment and deception. There were other pressures which convinced many colonists that they were fighting against increasing odds in their struggle to preserve their identity and way of life.

One cause for anxiety was the growth of the non-Welsh element in Chubut. Already much of the trade within the colony had passed into the hands of Argentine citizens and Italian immigrants who had found their way to Patagonia. This had resulted in some intermarriage between the Welsh and the newcomers which was accepted as inevitable. What seriously alarmed the community was the news that the Government had decided to sanction a scheme for the Italian colonization of part of Chubut. A company started by Senor Tarnassi, an Italian lawyer resident in Buenos Aires, was granted 200,000 acres of land which the Government had reserved for itself. A Presidential decree of February 14, 1901, gave official backing to the project, which envisaged the settlement of 280 Italian families near Lake Colwapi to the south of the Chubut valley. What may have affected the Welsh more than the grant itself was the element of discrimination in it. For whereas the Italians were to occupy the new land as an ethnic unit, the Welsh were not permitted by the Argentine authorities to acquire contiguous plots of fresh territory in Patagonia, but only mixed lots shared between colonists of different nationalities. (65)

Other fears and grievances fed the flames of frustration and discontent. The arrival of troops at Trelew convinced many colonists that there would be a stricter enforcement of compulsory military service, and, in fact, the bill for its general application throughout the Republic was approved by Congress before the end of 1901. There was much criticism also of the lack of proper medical care and facilities, and of the alleged meretricious behaviour of the two Argentine practitioners, one an Italian by birth and both non-Welsh speaking, who ministered to the colony. (66) The painfully slow procedure in the granting of title deeds of lands was, of course, a perennial complaint, and it was not made the more tolerable by the knowledge that the colonists were powerless to effect any change in the attitude of the Government. What was, perhaps, more reprehensible in the eyes of many of them was that it induced some of their number to take out Argentine citizenship in order to avoid the possibility of eviction, or to confirm their ownership of land. (67)

No less conducive to a feeling of insecurity amongst the colonists was their diminishing confidence in the ability, or even willingness, of the Argentine authorities to administer justice impartially and to maintain law and order. Chubut had been singularly free from the worst sort of outrages experienced in the other provinces of the Republic, but an event in the late months of 1900 signalled that the long period of immunity might be drawing to a close. What occurred not only roused the fears and suspicions of the Welsh, but revealed the existence of dissension and corruption within the higher ranks of local officialdom which had repercussions in Buenos Aires.

For fifteen years a Welsh colonist, John Morley, had steadily built up a flourishing farm at Trelew where he specialized in breeding cattle and sheep. But towards the end of 1900 a band of thieves headed by a notorious brigand, Benjamin Artiles, raided the farm, stole the stock and practically ruined Morley. His appeal to the judicial authorities in Rawson fell on deaf ears, and in his exasperation he sent a telegram to the British Legation in Buenos Aires, in which he ventilated his complaint and accused Pedro Martinez, the Chief of Police, Dr Alvarez, the Government Assessor and others of conniving at this and similar thefts of cattle by Artiles, and protecting him against the rigours of the law. (68) Clarke, the British Chargé d'Affaires, had no doubts about the seriousness of the case. He addressed a note on the subject to the Minister for Foreign Affairs, and called on President Roca to request an immediate investigation. The President shared his misgivings and promptly ordered the Ministry of the Interior to make the requisite inquiries.

A swift rejoinder to Morley's indictment came from Senor Conesa who had replaced O'Donnell as Governor of Chubut. He dismissed them as insubstantial and described the theft of a bull by Artiles as an "insignificant act." What is more, he informed the Minister of the Interior that the brigand had been arrested, but had been declared not guilty of the charges preferred against him by Morley, and released. (69)

It was now that a storm blew up in Chubut which converted a not uncommon act of cattle rustling into a local political issue. The Secretary of the Government of Chubut, Dr. Basaldua, who was known to be at daggers drawn with Conesa, allowed himself to be interviewed, and a full account of his observations on the Morley case was published in the Buenos Aires newspaper, the *Standard,* on January 15, 1901. After contrasting the intrepid qualities of the Welsh colonists with what he called the torpidity of the Governor, Basaldua openly associated the Chief of Police with the malpractices of Artiles and his band, and roundly declared that only the appointment of an honest and intelligent Governor in Conesa's place could rectify the situation before it got out of hand. (70) Such censorious statements were an open invitation for further comment by the metropolitan Press. The *Nacion* found it an opportune moment to publish revelations about the corrupt administration at Chubut. Other papers talked ominously of adverse consequences to the colony, such as the refusal of would-be immigrants to settle in Chubut, if the law continued to be flouted with impunity. The Argentine Government concurred to the extent of deciding to dispatch a commission to examine and report on conditions at first hand. (71)

In Chubut itself the colony had inevitably been affected by the cross-currents of personal views and political animosities. There was general agreement that Basaldua had been actuated by his own grievances in his attempt to discredit the Governor, and a small minority was prepared to testify to Conesa's irreproachable conduct and to the integrity of his subordinates. However, those who were concerned with the problem of preserving the Welsh character of the colony must have been profoundly distressed by one particular comment made by Basaldua in his interview. In reply to a question as to whether the Welsh in Chubut were hostile to the Republic, he had retorted with these words: "The Welsh! Why, they do not exist. To employ the word Welsh in reference to the present honourable settlers of the territory of the Chubut is an abuse of words. They are all Argentines down there." (72)

It was evident that, whatever the differences between Basaldua and Governor Conesa and their respective henchmen, they were united in disregarding or belittling those distinctions in language, culture and political background which infused and directed the thoughts and actions of the majority of the colonists. And the manner in which some of the latter were reacting to such anti-Welsh sentiments was suddenly shown to have taken a form other than restrained protest or silent resentment. For Basaldua had followed up his comment with an impassioned plea that, " it is necessary to stop the exodus of these desirable people to the Transvaal which has commenced since the Government was placed in the hands of Mr. Conesa."

The fact was that, imperceptibly at first but with gathering momentum, the idea of abandoning Chubut had sped up and down the valley. A year before, in 1900, Commander Groome of H.M.S. *Flora,* on a visit to Chubut, had been asked whether the British Government would require settlers in South Africa after the end of the Boer War. He had guardedly refused to answer the question, but had commented in his report that, "it seems a pity that when they (the Welsh) emigrated in 1865, they did not go to one of our colonies."(73) The chaplain of the *Flora,* the Reverend David Richards, a Welshman, was considerably less reticent in the report which he compiled and submitted to Sir William Barrington, the British Minister at Buenos Aires, and which Barrington transmitted to the British Government. Richards asserted that as many as 75 per cent of the colonists wished to leave Chubut, an estimate which was challenged by later naval and British embassy visitors.(74)

What could not be called into question, however, was the deliberation with which the possibilities of emigration were being explored by the colonists. In the early months of 1901 an Emigration Movement Committee was set up and William Lewis, a farmer and a keen imperialist, appointed as secretary. One hundred and fifty settlers expressed their firm intention to remove their families from Chubut, their names were forwarded to the British Legation in Buenos Aires, and it was confidently stated that a similar number would follow in a second wave of emigration. (75) Amongst them were many of the most influential men in the colony, who in the opinion of one resident, had every reason to believe that the ultimate aim of the Argentine administration was "overflooding and strangling every whit of British element from the hearts of the rising sons and daughters of Chubut." (76)

To establish a Welsh colony under the British flag in another part of the Empire was the avowed aim of the Emigration Committee. But it did not meet with the approval of all the colonists in Chubut. Those Welshmen who had become local officials or were storekeepers and railway employees were critical of the movement on the grounds that emigration would destroy the social and religious fabric of the community. A number of farmers and artisans were also satisfied with their lot, and feared the influx of alien immigrants who might prove to be indifferent argriculturists. This opposition, however, made little impact on the determination of the Emigration Committee to implement its plans which, towards the end of 1901, had narrowed down to a choice between Canada and South Africa as the two countries which offered the best prospects for the foundation of a Welsh colony. Moreover, the Committee anticipated that the Chubut emigrants would be assisted, at least in the initial stages of their removal, by the colonial authorities and the British Government itself.

It was at this moment that Mr W.J.Rees, of Swansea, and Mr. W. L. Griffith, of Cardiff, both agents of the Canadian Government, arrived in Chubut.(77)

PART 2

Call from Canada

I

For some years the Canadian Government had included Wales amongst those countries from which it hoped to attract a good proportion of desirable settlers to cultivate the virginal lands of its North-West Territories. It had no illusions as to the fierce competition it would encounter from other developing countries like the United States, the Argentine and various British colonies, which were also eager to tap the reservoir of emigrating European peoples. Much depended, of course, on the special concessions and liberal conditions offered in the free market of migrant Europeans, and, in this respect, Ottowa did not lag behind its rivals.

As far as Wales was concerned, there appeared to be two difficulties in the way of predisposing its inhabitants in favour of emigration. One was that, despite the high rents, the restricted number of farms available for purchase or lease-hold, and poor returns for hard work, the deeply rooted attachment of the rural population to the soil could not be broken, and their thoughts turned to emigration, without very strong inducements. The other was the expansion of industry which provided work and wages for any surplus agricultural labour, and which was soon to enjoy a fresh stimulus from the South African War. It was estimated, for instance, in 1899 that out of 120,000 miners in the Principality, no less than 60,000 were former smallholders and farm hands. (1) As long as this state of affairs continued, the prospect of recruiting emigrants for the distant prairies of Canada seemed to be very slim.

One person who refused to be discouraged by the outlook was W. L. Griffith, the emigration agent for the Canadian Government, who had already initiated more than one scheme to persuade reluctant Welshmen to try their fortunes in

Canada. It was he who had recommended that influential public figures in Wales should be invited by Ottowa to visit the North-West Territories, in the hope that they would be sufficiently impressed to extol their resources and potentialities to their countrymen at home. He had suggested the names of David Lloyd George, M.P. for Caernarvon Borough, W.J.Rees, a former Mayor of Swansea, and W. Llywelyn Williams, the distinguished barrister from Cardiff, as being prominent enough to win a respectful hearing for any cause advocated by them. The Canadian authorities had acted promptly, and in the autumn of 1899 the party found themselves touring through Manitoba, Assiniboia, Saskatchewan and British Columbia. Because of rumours of trouble in the Transvaal, Lloyd George decided to cut short his visit and return to London to attack the war policy of the Government. But a report on the tour was compiled and well publicized, some 15,000 copies in English and Welsh being distributed at the Royal Agricultural Show in Cardiff in 1901. The report spoke highly of the fecundity of the soil in Western Canada, and although it referred to certain climatic and social drawbacks, it undoubtedly helped to kindle a general interest in the advantages of emigrating to Canada. (2)

In looking around for prospective emigrants wherever they could be unearthed, Griffith could not fail to hear of the unhappy situation in Chubut, and he was probably instrumental in opening direct correspondence between the Canadian authorities and the colonists there. The appearance of Llwyd ap Iwan and Benbow Phillips in London gave him the opportunity he needed to inquire into the disposition of the settlers to opt for Canada. The interviews given by the two delegates and, later, the news of the devastation caused by the floods, reinforced his belief that Canada stood to gain from the mood of despondency in Chubut if acceptable offers were made to the colonists. "These facts," he wrote to Ottowa, "together with certain advances that have been made on their behalf lead to the conclusion that a large number of them are disposed to emigrate to Canada. It seems quite certain they would be a most desirable acquisition." (3)

However, eighteen months were to elapse before Griffith could feel that he was making some progress. The fact was that in any scheme for the removal of the Chubut Welsh to Canada, it was imperative to enlist the active sympathy of the British Government. But for the moment the Government had its hands full with the Boer War. What is more, the Colonial Office, under the firm guidance of Joseph Chamberlain, was immersed in his policy of a massive colonization of the disaffected Boer territories which were in the process of being occupied by the British forces. It was rumoured that between 30,000 and 40,000 of the volunteers and reserves in South Africa would be retained there for this purpose after the war. Then on June 25, 1900, the *Times* published an article which argued forcefully in favour of state-aided colonization, and mentioned the sum of £10,000 as a first step in that direction. It justified such expenditure on the grounds that without a majority of loyalist settlers it would not be possible for Britain to govern the newly acquired provinces in South Africa. (4)

With one powerful Government department and an influential national organ conceding priority to the cause of South African emigration, Griffith may have felt that the voice of Canada would merely raise a faint echo in the corridors of Whitehall. But his cause too had its protagonists. The *Times* article was challenged in an outspoken letter by T.R.Preston, the Inspector of Canadian Agencies in Europe. In his view, it was questionable politics to force a British population on the South African *veldt* in order to enable the Government to administer and control the Transvaal and Orange Free State. He deplored the implication that Britain was incapable of ruling a colony unless the majority of its people were British, particularly as the true test and genius of government lay in ruling an adverse majority with a kindly hand. In Canada, although the British element was in a minority, the population as a whole was loyal to Britain. To ignore the claims of that progressive and liberal-minded colony on would-be British emigrants was therefore untimely. But what was demonstrably invidious was the competition that Canada would have to face if the British Government sponsored state-aided emigration to South Africa, when both justice and self-interest demanded that all the colonies of the British Empire should benefit from it. (5)

These were persuasive arguments which did not go unnoticed in the Colonial Office. At the same time more vociferous support came from Wales where the Press, led by the *Western Mail,* whose editor was a good friend of Griffith's, came out strongly in favour of emigration to Canada. The *Western Mail* identified itself so closely with the campaign as to send a special investigator to report on conditions in Canada, and his favourable articles were widely read throughout the Principality. (6)

It was towards the end of the summer of 1901 that Griffith saw some hope of bringing his scheme to fruition, when the Colonial Office momentarily relaxed its gaze on South Africa. A memorandum from that Office hinted that the reason was an unexpected hitch. After recalling that there had been talk the previous year of removing some Chubut settlers to Canada, it went on to say: "Let us facilitate their doing so as the South African project seems rather in the clouds and Lord Milner seems to have made no proposal." (7) Whatever the reason, Chamberlain appeared to be more ready to examine the feasibility of transporting settlers from Chubut, and from that moment events moved quickly. It was arranged that the Canadian High Commissioner in London should be provided with the latest Admiralty report on the colony, on the condition that he treated it as a confidential document. Furthermore, upon his request for a private interview with the chaplain of the *Flora,* Rev. D. Richards, no objection was raised although the reverend gentleman's views had not exactly recommended him to the British Government as an unimpeachable source of information.*

At this point Griffith exchanged propaganda for action. He made arrangements to visit Patagonia in order to confer with

* *See* Notes, Chapter 1, No. 74.

the Chubut Emigration Committee, and to discuss the project of moving to Canada with as many settlers as possible. He also showed both foresight and wisdom by inviting W. J. Rees to accompany him on the mission. The presence and loquacity of a notable Welshman of the day, who had toured the North-West Territories with Lloyd George in 1899 would, he thought, add conviction and colour to what he himself could only adumbrate in terms of material inducements. Rees willingly agreed, and the date of departure was fixed for August 22, 1901.

The British Government gave them not only its blessing, but some valuable diplomatic assistance as well. A hurried correspondence between the Colonial Office, the Foreign Office and the Canadian High Commissioner resulted in a decision that the British Legation in Buenos Aires should be directed to provide all possible facilities and help for the two visitors. For good measure, it was suggested that a member of the Legation should be attached to the mission. It was a comforting thought for Griffith and Rees that, in any eventuality, they could count on something more tangible than mere official good wishes. (8)

II

The mission arrived in Buenos Aires in the third week of September and there were immediate consultations between the two delegates and the British Minister, Barrington. Since land communications with Chubut were out of the question, arrangements were concluded for them to travel by boat, and Scott, the Secretary of the British Embassy, was delegated to accompany them. One preliminary matter which had to be settled was whether it would be opportune at that stage to notify the Argentine Government of the object of the visit, and here the visitors preferred to be advised by Barrington. "I thought it advisable to mention the intended journey to the Minister for Foreign Affairs. I had previously discussed the expediency of so doing with them, and after reflection they agreed with me that it would be quite impossible to conceal their visit to Chubut and its object, and that it would be prudent to forestall any reports probably of exaggerated import which otherwise might reach this Government, in the first instance from that place, and which would on this account perhaps cause a disagreeable impression which it would be well to avoid as far as possible. I therefore explained the circumstances briefly at an interview I had with the Minister, saying that it was proposed to see what could be done to relieve such of the settlers who were discontented with their lot." (9)

Whatever the private feelings of the Argentine Minister of Foreign Affairs, his attitude was one of courtesy and helpfulness, which was reflected later in the collaboration of the Argentine Department of Marine. It arranged passages for the mission on the ship *Guardia Nacional,* and throughout the voyage Griffith and Rees were hospitably entertained by its commander. They disembarked at Port Madryn on October 5, and proceeded by train to Trelew where they were accorded an enthusiastic welcome by the settlers.

One misapprehension required to be removed before any problem could be ventilated by colonists and delegates. The latter were made aware of it when they paid a courtesy call on Governor Conesa, who had travelled from Rawson to Trelew. For some reason the Argentine officials in Chubut were inclined to think that the two Canadian commissioners had been involved in the activities of Llwyd ap Iwan and Benbow Phillips in London two years previously. Following this train of thought they were convinced that the purpose of the mission was to devise a scheme for the eventual establishment of a British Protectorate over Chubut.(10) These suspicions were successfully disposed of, but they revealed the ineradicable distrust felt by Argentine officialdom of any foreigners who enquired too closely into affairs within the colony.

The next five weeks were spent by Griffith and Rees in ascertaining the feelings and wishes of the settlers. One inescapable fact that emerged from their investigations was that the contending pro-and anti-emigration parties were fairly evenly matched, and had a profusion of arguments to support their respective points of view.

On the one hand, the effects of the floods in 1900 and 1901 had shaken the economy of the colony to its very roots. The value of farms had fallen, few of the irrigation canals could be put to practical use, and the corresponding decrease in the acreage of land sown with wheat threatened the livelihood of many of the settlers, some of whom were now dependent on public relief. The mere fact that £20,000 was owed by the community to the Mercantile Company of Chubut, which transported exportable grain to Buenos Aires, was evidence enough of the impoverished state of the colony. To escape from the demoralization and depression of a half-ruined economy must have offered the only hope of salvation to those who had suffered most.

On the other hand there was a strong body of opinion that held tenaciously to the belief that the colonists should stand their ground, and that the Argentine Government would assist them in restoring their economy. It was pointed out with some justification that official quarters had done much to alleviate distress in the form of grants of money and the suspension of customs duties at Port Madryn. Something more substantial, it was said, could be expected particularly after President Roca had telephoned to Lloyd Jones, an influential preacher in the valley, requesting him to urge the colonists not to emigrate. It was confidently anticipated that this intervention would strengthen the opposition against any exodus from Chubut, although Jones had roused some scepticism by taking out Argentine naturalization papers.

There was also the additional friction of opposing attitudes within the pro-emigration party itself, many of whom showed a distinct preference for South Africa rather than Canada. In this atmosphere of controversy, doubt and criticism, the two Canadian commissioners adopted the only reliable method of establishing how many settlers were desirous of going to Canada. Forms were distributed inviting their signatures, and the results must have given immense satisfaction to Griffith. Two hundred and sixty people signed them, and these included fifty heads of families and twenty six young men over eighteen years of age. Moreover, another two hundred signified their intention of following in the wake of the first group of emigrants. (11) They all expressed the hope that the British Government would assist them to meet the expenses of their passage and the transport of their stock. Griffith could not commit himself on this point, but he could legitimately congratulate himself that as far as his own expenses to Chubut were concerned, they had been amply justified by the success of his mission. (12)

It was found impracticable to discuss the question of transport with the Canadian Government by cable, and the commissioners were obliged to return to Buenos Aires to do so. Before leaving Chubut they made every effort to ensure that there would be no vacillation or withdrawal amongst the intending emigrants. Both parties agreed that the most favourable month for the removal to Canada would be April, 1902; a local committee was formed to act as liaison between the emigrants and the two commissioners; and finally, the former undertook to set aside a sum of money or some stock as security for their *bona fide* intention of moving to Canada.

With five hundred prospective emigrants in hand Griffith could indulge in sanguine expectations that his plans would not be thwarted by the financial stringency of government departments in Ottowa and London, and might well evoke sympathetic support from the Welsh public, once the facts had been made known to it. For the colony the prospect of losing so many people could only be interpreted as the first serious step towards its disintegration. What is, perhaps, remarkable is that not one of the settlers, when faced with the question of whether to abandon Chubut to emigrate elsewhere, so much as hinted that he would like to return to Wales. (13)

III

Considering the enormous distance involved and the time required for communication between the parties, six months seemed a very short interval for finalizing transport and reception arrangements between Chubut and Canada. But as soon as Griffith arrived home, he set about to galvanize the Welsh public into making an effective demonstration on behalf of the emigrants. This, he hoped, would help to extract some concession from the British Government, preferably in the form of free shipping.

What followed was one of the most interesting newspaper campaigns in the history of the Welsh Press, with the *Western Mail* prominently in the van. In one vibrant or pungent article after another, the paper declared that it was a matter of national concern that the Chubut Welsh should be extricated from what it described as "a state which is, if not one of actual, at least of practical serfdom." It spoke of the colony's long years of unrelenting struggle against the adversities of climate and Argentine administration; of the inextinguishable loyalty of the settlers to the British flag, "the value of which they have learned to appreciate during their years of exile"; and of the desire of the majority of the settlers to abandon "a hopelessly discredited experiment." It insisted that the problem of their removal to Canada transcended all party and sectional interests, and required concerted action within the Principality and collaboration from the Government on moral and humanitarian grounds. (14)

Sympathy for the colonists did not end at the Welsh border. In a matter of a few days the story of the hardships and difficulties of the Chubut community had become the common property of newspapers throughout the kingdom. Editorial comment was fairly uniform as to the desirability of rescuing them from the error of their ways which had planted them in the shadow of an alien flag. The *Yorkshire Post* was apparently moved by the thought that the Argentine Government was now teaching "soft Spanish to children accustomed to regard vowels with contempt, strongly nurtured in the terrific gutterals and formidable double consonants of Adam and Owen Glendower." (15) In the opinion of the *Standard,* "the Welsh Colony in Patagonia will deserve to live in the history of Colonial misadventures besides Law's Scottish Darien scheme." Quoting Griffith's remark that, "if they (the colonists) had been Englishmen they would probably have drifted helplessly, and if they had been Scotsmen they would have contrived to get away," the paper commended the settlers for their qualities of endurance and courage which could be put to better use "on the soil of Greater Britain."(16) In a more magisterial frame of mind the *Daily Telegraph* concluded that, "if any lesson for emigrants emerges from the experiences of the Welsh settlers in South America, it is the practical, as well as the patriotic, wisdom of following the flag." (17)

But with whatever aspect of the situation they chose to deal, and with due recognition of the assistance given by the Argentine Government on the material plane, it was evident that the English like the Welsh Press understood the fundamental reasons for the proposed move from Chubut. And they understood them to be an inherent dislike for compulsory military service, an unshakeable attachment to their traditional way of life and their particular creed and speech, and the now passionate conviction that these could be better preserved in a British colony than in Patagonia.

Concurrently with this vigorous Press campaign came the news that the Canadian Government had publicized the details of its scheme for the resettlement of the colonists. The concessions were of a nature to appeal to people who were intent on conserving the communal life and those cultural and religious affinities to which they were inured.

The Government in Ottawa undertook to reserve a complete township of 36 square miles at a place to be selected by the colonists or their representatives for the purposes of the proposed Welsh colony. A special staff would be appointed to accompany, locate and advise the emigrants upon their arrival in Canada. The Canadian authorities also assumed the entire responsibility of providing accommodation for two or three months while the settlers were building their own houses. Finally, they offered a money grant in the form of a bonus of £1 per head (men, women and children) to the Welsh Patagonian Committee in Wales which was acting on behalf of the Chubut Welsh. (18)

These terms, described as generous and magnanimous by certain papers, guaranteed a permanent home for the emigrants with all the advantages of security and benevolence under the British flag. But there still remained the problem of transport and its expenses which could not be met by the resources of the colonists, nor by the money grant of the Canadian Government. To persuade the British Government to play its part in the implementation of the scheme, and to ensure its success by agreeing to convey the emigrants to Canada, was the next and indispensable step. Already the supporters of the emigration project in Wales were mustering their forces to bring the strongest pressure they could bear on the man in whose hands lay the decision - the Colonial Secretary, Joseph Chamberlain.

IV

The spearhead of the movement for the removal of the Chubut Welsh was the Welsh Patagonian Committee, whose members were drawn from the most influential industrial, parliamentary and local government circles. Irrespective of party affiliations and religious and social differences within the Principality, they were deeply concerned with the disabilities and privations of their countrymen in Patagonia, and unanimous in their view that repatriation was the rightful solution. Humanitarian reasons alone were enough to justify Government action in helping the scattered and defenceless flock in Chubut to return to the British fold. But it was also incontestably true that such a body of industrious and courageous settlers should not be allowed to waste their energies on the arid soil of Patagonia when so many fertile regions within the British Empire were calling for experienced and loyal colonists. On both moral and practical grounds, the Welsh Patagonian Committee felt that it was armed with unassailable arguments when it asked the Colonial Secretary to receive a deputation. The thought that they would be dealing with the dedicated architect of Imperial colonization must have encouraged its members in their belief that their mission would be fruitful, and the relatively small matter of providing transport for the Chubut emigrants - the cardinal object of the meeting - settled with little difficulty.

The deputation which met Chamberlain and other high-ranking officials of the Colonial Office on February 18, 1902, was imposingly large (some 66 in number), and representative of all shades of Welsh political and religious life. (19) One after another their spokesmen rose to unfold the tragic history of the Chubut settlement, and to stress the urgency of liberating a group of intrepid and loyal British subjects from a situation made intolerable by natural disasters and the interference of an alien administration.

Alfred Thomas, the Secretary of the Welsh Parliamentary Party, who led the deputation, expatiated on the remarkable achievements of the colonists in the past, and drew a pathetic picture of their present distress. Despite the construction of schemes of irrigation that "literally made a waste desert to blossom like a rose," the colony now lay derelict in the wake of the floods. But what to the colonists was more revolting than any calamity that could be brought upon them by the forces of Nature was the constant interference of the Argentine Government with their social and religious environments. For these reasons they were turning their eyes "to the old flag that had never failed to help and succour any Briton wherever he might be stranded and under whatever circumstances." The settlers had eagerly accepted the Canadian Government's offer of land and means of subsistence. They now appealed through the deputation "to Mr. Chamberlain to become the Joshua who would lead them to the promised land."

The speech by William Jones M.P was an even more impassioned tribute to the loyalist qualities of the Chubut Welsh, and a pertinent reminder that such attributes of devotion to British traditions were precisely what the Colonial Secretary needed in the prosecution of his colonizing policy. "If the right honourable gentleman could help them to tide over their difficulties, he would not merely be helping people who had been in storm and stress, but would be helping also to build what he had so much at heart, Britain's great Empire, and make it greater for the future welfare of the world."

Other members of the deputation spoke in the same vein, and it was left to W.L.Griffith and W.J.Rees, who were personally acquainted with the circumstances of the colonists, to elaborate on the more practical aspects of the proposed emigration. Rees confined himself to his own assessment of the poor material prospects which faced the colony, and which explained why five hundred Chubut Welsh were anxious to make a fresh start in Canada. Sensing, perhaps, that too much emphasis on the poverty of the community might create the unfortunate impression that the Colonial Office was being asked to assist a crowd of penniless and importunate men, he made it quite clear that, on the contrary, the emigrants were ready to meet the expenses of removal by having whatever money was spent by the Government on their transportation treated as a charge on the land taken up by them in Canada.

Griffith, for his part, underlined this point of the solvency of the emigrants who, he affirmed, could dispose of their farms or effects by sale. He went on to make two shrewd comments calculated to warm the hearts of his listeners. The non-Welsh inhabitants of Chubut had been much impressed by the solicitude shown by the British Government for its subjects in that remote valley of Patagonia. Moreover, if the emigrants were afforded transport by the Government to make their way to Canada, he had little doubt that the effect would be to divert a stream of Welsh settlers from the United States to that country, where they were generally regarded as the most desirable of all emigrants.

Finally, Gwilym Lewis, himself a former settler who had spent 26 years in Patagonia, recapitulated the motives which lay behind the wish to move to Canada, and closed the case for the emigrants by directing his final words to the Colonial Secretary. "I can assure you that there are no more loyal Britishers in the world than the Welsh settlers in Chubut, and most of their political troubles arise from the fact that they refuse to sink their British citizenship."

Chamberlain had listened to the perorations and arguments with every indication of deep interest, interpolating occasional questions which elicited the information *inter alia* that conveying the settlers from Chubut to Canada would cost over £5000, and double that sum if stock and horses were also transported by sea.

The opening remarks of the Colonial Secretary were reassuring enough, for he too applauded the allegiance of the Patagonian Welsh to the country of their origin, and their in-

domitable energy in overcoming obstacles. A slightly depreca-
tory manner in passing over the political grievances of the
colonists may have caused some people present to raise their
eyebrows. But the whole deputation must have been disconcerted by the blunt statement that followed.

It was to the effect that the Colonial Secretary had received
its members under a misapprehension. He had assumed that
the Chubut Welsh were desirous of finding a new home in the
recently established Crown Colonies in South Africa, in which
case it would have been his pleasurable duty to examine the
means of helping them to acquire suitable land and smoothing
over initial difficulties. "Certainly I should rejoice very much
to have a colony of Welshmen, or loyal Welshmen, established
in South Africa." The Chubut emigrants, however, had stated
their preference for Canada, and that, Chamberlain declared,
"puts me in a position in which I am powerless to assist your
object." He explained that the British Government had long
ceased to subsidize any form of emigration to self-governing
colonies like Canada, preferring to respect their independence
of action in such questions. To depart from this policy by
creating a precedent in the case of the Patagonian Welsh would
necessitate the adoption of a new principle, and that was a
matter for the Prime Minister and the Government. Besides,
the latter, and the Colonial Office in particular, had no money
for the purpose required by the deputation.

Having disposed of its request, the Colonial Secretary
proferred some advice to the disconsolate deputation. The
Canadian Government could be approached again and asked
to review, and possibly augment, its grant or offer a loan to the
emigrants. If this approach produced no result, the funds
required could be raised by public subscription which,
Chamberlain firmly believed, would meet with a generous
response outside as well as inside Wales.

After this there remained nothing for the deputation to do
except thank the Colonial Secretary and withdraw. (2) But its
members did not disperse and go their separate ways with
heavy hearts. Within a few hours they reassembled in the Hotel

Victoria and decided, without a dissentient voice, to translate words into action and put their patriotism and that of their countrymen to the test of organizing a fund to meet the expenses of the removal to Canada. An announcement that the Colonial Secretary himself was eager to contribute to such a cause created an upsurge of liberality amongst all members of the delegation, who between them donated £1400. After this auspicious start the fund was thrown open to the Welsh public, with every expectation that, as the Bishop of St. David's fervently hoped, Wales would rally round the promoters of the scheme and display to the world a subscription worthy of the Principality.

V

The somewhat passive resignation of the delegation to the Colonial Secretary's rejection of the request for free transport for the Chubut Welsh stood out in contrast to the criticism that his attitude provoked in a number of newspapers. The idea that a dominant naval power like Britain could not provide a vessel to convey a few hundred emigrants to Canada patently annoyed the *Belfast Evening Telegraph* which asked: "Are there no ships in the Royal navy that could be utilized for the purpose?. . .Cannot the old country provide the trifling cost of removal? It is possible for red-tapeism to go a shade too far."(21) The *St. James's Gazette* was frankly censorious of the policy which inhibited the Government from assisting emigration to self-governing colonies, and which Chamberlain had invoked to justify his refusal of aid in the case of the Patagonian Welsh. "We trust that the incident will set the Colonial Office thinking as to the possibility of coming to some agreement with the Governments of the self-governing Colonies by which, while the latter retain the right of specifying what stamp of immigrant it is that they are willing to receive, the Home Government will be prepared to give reasonable aid to settlers of the right stamp who shall be willing to go." (22)

Freeman's Journal of Dublin chose to take the Colonial Secretary to task for scarcely concealing the preferential treatment that he was prepared to give to settlers intending to emigrate to South Africa rather than any other British colony. As regards the Chubut emigrants: "How could such a people settle in the Transvaal? First of all, like the Boers themselves, they would want to speak their own tongue, and it is well known that if Chamberlain and Lord Milner had their way such a thing will not be allowed, the only language to be recognized under the new regime being the English. The Welshmen went to Patagonia half a century ago *(sic)* that they might be able to lead the life they most cared about. That is surely impossible in the South Africa of today."(23)

What mystified not a few people was Chamberlain's admission that he had somehow come to associate the delegation of the Welsh Patagonian Committee with a proposal for transporting the Chubut settlers to South Africa. The most charitable explanation was that his preoccupation with South African matters had led him to assume that, when the case of the Chubut emigrants had been presented to him initially, he had connected it in some way with the new colonies of the Transvaal and Orange Free State. That hard-working ministers like Chamberlain could become confused on occasions was perfectly intelligible to public opinion in Britain, but rather less so in Canada. There national pride was distinctly hurt by the report that the Colonial Secretary was unable to help the Patagonian Welsh to move to Canada, but was willing to send them to South Africa. An irate Press disapproved of such discrimination in forthright language, and declared it to be a poor return for the role played by Canadian soldiers in the Boer War. Not the least mordant in its comment on this point was the principal French newspaper in Canada, which chose to remind Chamberlain that loyalty, while a good thing, could sometimes become a very onerous burden. (24)

The Colonial Secretary was greatly disturbed by the Canadian reaction which he attributed to a misconception of what he had really said to the delegation of the Welsh Patagonian Committee. That the misunderstanding was due to an imperfectly summarized version of his speech he himself had no doubt, and a full report would quickly clear it up. What was less defensible, in many men's opinion, was the reason that could give rise to a misinterpretation or misrepresentation of this kind, and which indubitably was Chamberlain's excessive partiality for South African colonization. He was not allowed to forget it, and an oblique reference to it could occasionally ruffle his composure in the House of Commons. This happened when D. A. Thomas rose to ask him whether his suggestion to the delegation that the Patagonian settlers might go to a warmer climate than that of Canada, was limited to South Africa. Chamberlain was visibly nettled and retorted sharply that if the question was meant to be a joke, it was a very bad one and that he declined to answer it. (25)

VI

But already there were misgivings in Wales about the Canadian scheme. News had arrived that the Argentine Government had offered the Chubut colonists land in another and reputedly more fertile region of the Republic, and that consequently much of the initial enthusiasm for emigrating to Canada had evaporated. The offer amounted to 100 farms of 240 acres each on the island of Choele Coel, which lay up the Rio Negro, some three hundred miles north of Trelew. The Government also promised a grant of 50,000 dollars towards building a canal along the whole length of the island in order to counteract the effects of the floods which were more frequent there than in Chubut. Meetings had been held in Trelew, Rawson and Gaiman to consider the proposal, and although the discussions had proved inconclusive, it was believed that two hundred people, most of them young married couples without farms, would leave for Rio Negro in the near future. (26)

If this was a disconcerting report for the promoters of the Canadian scheme, more was to follow. News published by Reuters that, "the majority of the Welsh settlers in the Chubut district have informed the authorities that they have no thought of leaving the country" was confirmed by the Foreign Office during question time in the House of Commons. (27) These statements conflicted with the facts of the case presented to Chamberlain by the delegation of the Welsh Patagonian Committee. As some Welsh papers were quick to point out, they could not only confuse the public in Wales as to the actual state of affairs in Chubut, but check the flow of subscriptions to the Emigration Fund and so jeopardize the whole project. One paper, at least, was inclined to detect the hand of the

Argentine Government in the dissemination of such information. (28)

Some of the fears of the pro-Canada Press were soon realized. Doubts were raised whether Canada, or South Africa for that matter, was the sole alternative to be considered. An unexpected new suggestion was put forward that British Guiana, the only British possession on the South American continent, might be a more felicitous solution to the Chubut problem. The climate of that colony was salubrious, it was one of the richest "undeveloped estates of the Crown", and its greatest need was white settlers. The change from the banks of the Chubut to the "fertile regions of the Upper Essequibo or Demerara" would be "one from chaos and desolation to a sunny land teeming with riches." (29)

A greater source of anxiety to the Welsh Patagonian Committee than exhilarating but vague propositions of this kind, was the fact that its exertions in promoting the cause of Canadian emigration had not passed without some criticism and protest in Wales. It would certainly have been strange if the divergences of opinion on the subject in Patagonia itself had not found protagonists amongst those former settlers who had returned to their homeland, but kept up a constant correspondence with their kinsfolk and friends in Chubut. The views of one section which opposed the Canadian scheme were forcefully represented in a letter to the Press. It warned the Committee that it was acting only for a handful of disaffected colonists and not for the settlement as a whole, which had not the slightest inclination or wish to be "deported" to Canada. It denied the existence of any "Canadian fever" amongst the Chubut Welsh, and expostulated with the Committee for allowing itself to be misled by reports of abject misery and "serfdom" in Patagonia. "It is absolutely untrue, and exceedingly unkind, not to say cruel. The colonists have thousands of dear friends in Wales, whose feelings are needlessly harrowed by such representation. These outbreaks of disaffection occur in Chubut like strikes and lockouts in Wales." The Committee was advised also to refrain from reflecting unkindly on the

Argentine Government which had generously assisted the colonists in their distress. It was true that there were grievances like conscription, and that some Argentine officials were "Jacks-in-office and delight to apply the law in the most awkward and galling manner." But, the letter insisted, "we in this country (Britain) are fighting today for the religious and political liberty which they enjoy to the full in Chubut." (30)

In Bala, Merionethshire, where Michael D.Jones had first conceived of an independent Welsh colony, his son-in-law, the Reverend Thomas Rhys, professor in the Independent College of Bala-Bangor, was distressed at the thought that five hundred Chubut Welsh wished to emigrate to Canada. It was not the loss of so many able-bodied settlers to Chubut that perturbed him, for he had no quarrel with the notion of exchanging Patagonia for a more progressive British colony. He saw eye-to-eye with his brother-in-law Llwyd ap Iwan on that necessity, but was more favourably disposed towards South Africa. Apart from his partiality for the latter country, he was genuinely concerned about the notorious severity of Canadian winters and its possible lethal effect on people accustomed to the more temperate climate of Patagonia. "What can they (the emigrants) expect from a place like Canada but that they will succumb by the score or hundred even the first winter after settling?", (31) he wrote in one of his letters to Lyttelton Gell,* a director of the South Africa Company in Rhodesia, who was later to take a keen interest in the possibility of transferring the Chubut settlers to South Africa.

From the very beginning Rhys was sceptical of the optimistic reports of enthusiasm shown for the Canadian scheme which had been brought back from Chubut by W.L.Griffith and W.J.Rees. Neither had he much confidence in the judgment of the deputation which met Chamberlain. "I am given to understand that the deputation will meet Mr. Chamberlain tomorrow, Tuesday. I understand also that only a small number have given their names to the Canadian agents - some

* See *Infra* pp. 102.

400-500 - as intending to leave Chubut for Canada. If at all possible I believe the Colonial Secretary should be informed of the facts, so that he may not be misled by the deputation. I have no idea who has managed this affair of the deputation. The gentlemen appointed know hardly anything of the Chubut Colony and figure in connection with it now for the first time. The 400 settlers from Chubut who are bent on going to Canada I understand are men who have had no grants of land in Patagonia, and so the loss of them will not be much felt." (32)

It was a profound relief to Rhys to hear that Chamberlain had turned down the deputation's appeal for free transport, but it in no way reassured him that it would deflect W. L. Griffith and the Welsh Patagonian Committee from their declared purpose of forging ahead with their Canadian scheme. "What I fear now is that the Canadian Government will stir too soon and send a ship to Chubut immediately before we have time to lay our plans before the colonists with regard to their proposed removal to South Africa." (33) It was this possibility that may, perhaps, have led him to question the reliability of the data fed to the Committee by Griffith, and to regard his statements on Chubut as tendentious. Referring himself to a conversation with a Chubut colonist who had recently arrived in Wales, Evan E.Jones, he wrote that "hardly any of the four to five hundred men who gave their names at Chubut to the Canadian agents promised to go to Canada. The Canadian agents merely collected the names of those who stated that they were determined to leave Argentina. Mr. E.E.Jones avers that nearly all these men - the 4 to 5 hundred - prefer going to S.Africa rather than to any other British colony. They have signed no agreement at all with the Canadian agents, and the great majority of the men have no intention or wish to emigrate to Canada on account of the severity of the climate in winter. If this be the fact - which I, from my knowledge of Mr. Jones, cannot doubt for a moment - the two Canadian agents in their speeches before the meeting of the delegation to the Colonial Secretary must have somewhat misrepresented or wrongly coloured the real state of affairs as they found them in Chubut." (34).

The Welsh Patagonian Committee could not have been unaware of animadversions of this kind, and of the confusion
they might create in the minds of the public in Wales. It
probably felt confident enough to ignore them, but what could
not be dismissed as immaterial was the slow response to the
appeal for donations to the Emigration Fund. For despite the
prominent lead given by the Prince of Wales who sent £25, and
the generous gifts of others, only £700 had been contributed
during the three weeks since the Emigration Fund had been
launched on a wave of subscriptions amounting to £1400. The
lowest estimate for conveying the five hundred emigrants envisaged by W.L.Griffith was £5000 or a little more. It was
therefore evident that there would have to be a further appeal
or a modification of the Canadian scheme, if it were to be
implemented at all. This was the immediate question facing the
Welsh Patagonian Committee when it met in the boardroom of
the *Western Mail* on April 8, 1902.

As soon as the proceedings were formally opened,
W.L.Griffith submitted a report which had the effect of exor-
cising any doubts that those settlers, who had expressed a wish
to go to Canada, were now hesitant about doing so. On the
contrary, in the light of information and letters from Patagonia, Griffith was able to prove convincingly that there was
no defection in their ranks. The news of the efforts made on
their behalf at home had fortified their resolution. A well
attended meeting in Gaiman had endorsed once again the
decision to emigrate to Canada, and a few colonists had
managed to sell their farms and stock already, although at a
loss. What was more sensational, however, was the fact that
some forty Chubut Welsh, impatient of delay and in the happy
position of being able to pay for their own passages, had
arrived in Britain and were leaving Liverpool for Canada
within the next few days.

Impressed by this exhibition of "Canadian fever" the
Committee decided that no time should be lost in removing the
emigrants who had remained behind in Patagonia. With the
money in hand it was calculated that between 250 and 300

people could be conveyed to Canada. Griffith's affirmation that if these left Chubut the whole colony would eventually follow in their wake, was no doubt cautiously viewed by the Committee as smacking of euphoria. But it authorized him to make arrangements for a steamer to call at Chubut to take the first batch of emigrants at a through rate to Canada. It was also thought advisable to ask the local committee in Patagonia to make a selection of the most deserving cases amongst the settlers with a view to expediting the removal.

Besides executing these commissions the indefatigable Canadian agent travelled to Liverpool to supervize the embarkation of the forty Chubut emigrants already there. They had reached that port at a time when emigration from Britain to Canada was proceeding at an unparalleled rate, and two ships were leaving weekly packed with settlers. Room was found for them on the Allan Liner *Ionian,* but not before their presence amongst the milling crowds of emigrants had attracted much attention. "The Welsh Patagonians were a distinctive class - smart, well groomed and intelligent. Their physique, too, was that of the hardy, useful character so essential for successful colonization. Equally noticeable was their bright and happy demeanour, a pleasing contrast to the gloomy and somewhat sullen visages of most of the foreign emigrants. They betrayed no feeling of regret, but rather a joyous anticipation of the probability of having a fair chance of doing good and useful work as men and citizens in their new Canadian home. . .They were the admiration of the vast and motley crowd of people passing to and fro." (35) When they finally sailed on April 10, 1902, the group had the satisfaction, not only of receiving telegrams of good wishes from the Welsh Patagonian Committee, but also of being singled out by photographers on board the *Ionian.*

VII

Back from the festive atmosphere of Liverpool Griffith
discovered, to his chagrin, that any hope of transporting the
main body of the emigrants directly to Canada would have to
be abandoned. The Emigration Fund was inadequate to
finance such an ambitious scheme, and the Chubut Welsh
would, after all, have to put up with the inconvenience of the
long and circuitous voyage *via* Liverpool. This, of course,
meant that they would be unable to bring any stock with them,
an eventuality which many had hoped to avoid, and that they
would have to dispose of them as best they could. Inevitably
the consternation and disappointment that followed the
receipt of this news in Chubut must have dissuaded some
settlers from leaving. Nevertheless, the local committee was
able to cable Griffith at the end of April that 250 emigrants
were eager to avail themselves of the pecuniary assistance
offered by the Welsh Patagonian Committee.

In the meantime Griffith had entered into negotiations with
the Pacific Steam Navigation Company which ran a line of
Royal Mail steamers between Liverpool and the west coast of
South America. The Company agreed to transfer the settlers
from Port Madryn to Liverpool and thence to Quebec, and to
transport all subsequent parties of emigrants at the same rate,
even if they were fewer in number. (36) It was evident that
Griffith had not renounced his sanguine expectations that if
the first group settled down happily in Canada, the rest of the
Chubut community would become compulsive emigrants to
that Dominion.

Early in May, 1902, the Pacific Steam Navigation
Company's steamer *Orissa* put in at Port Madryn, and the
embarkation of the emigrants and their effects began

immediately. Unlike the departure of the Chubut Welsh from Liverpool at the beginning of the previous month, it was not entirely a happy occasion. Feelings over the exodus of so many hardy and irreplaceable colonists had run high during the preceding months, and some of the bitterness had percolated into the pages of Buenos Aires and Chubut newspapers. The metropolitan *Herald,* describing the embarkation itself, said that "the Welsh who went aboard the *Orissa* at Madryn had to deposit £5 each to ensure their going as far as Liverpool to take advantage of the free trip, and thence to Wales and back to Choele Choel. Many have left their goods and families behind. Most of them will return, it is said. The emigration is a fiasco." (37)

This was scarcely consonant with the facts, but it was a fairly mild observation compared with the vitriolic comments published in the *Drafod,* the organ of the colony, by the Reverend D.Lloyd Jones, who castigated the deputation of the Welsh Patagonian Committee for supporting the Canadian emigration movement. "Why in the name of all that is reasonable are not the Welsh people of Wales, who are daily under the influence of the deputation, who have been born and bred under the nourishing protection of the British flag, why are not they sufficiently loyal to go to "loyal" Canada to build the future of the Empire?" As to the meeting of the deputation with Chamberlain and the conduct of its members, "the whole of Wales had ordered a truce and general surrender and great silence for three quarters of an hour, each to be under penalty and pain unless he completely forgot Nonconformity, Radicalism and Pro-Boerism, the oppression of Court, Church and School, the arrogance of the lords of land, coal, slate and all minerals, together with the game and the fish of river and sea; unless he forgot the great suffering of the loyal Welsh poor of Great Britain and the troubles of Ireland; unless he forgot the widows and orphans of the killed in the Transvaal and the hundreds of thousands who die from hunger in India; unless he forgot all but the British flag and the deplorable conditions of the Welsh of the Camwy." But, the reverend gentleman insisted, such "deplorable conditions" were illusionary. There were no poor in Chubut, all settlers could make a living, the acreage of the valley was greater, and its average yield of corn better, than that of the territory to be set apart for the emigrants in Canada. He himself would not go to that country if ten thousand pounds were placed in his hand. "There was not anywhere under the sun a colony of Welshmen so well off, so independent, so free and so contented as the Welsh of the Camwy." (38)

Nevertheless, despite this hard-hitting denunciation of the Canadian scheme, some 234 colonists went aboard the *Orissa* which steamed out of Port Madryn on May 15, 1902. (39) The party consisted of 28 families, many of them with twelve or more children, who saw little hope for the younger generation to enjoy a prosperous life in Chubut. Before leaving each family deposited £5 as security which was to be reimbursed upon their arrival in Quebec. As the money subscribed in Britain to the Emigration Fund was only enough to pay for 160 passages, the more well-to-do emigrants renounced their claims in advance and agreed that their deposits should be used to defray the expenses of their less fortunate compatriots. (40) To those, and they were in the majority, who had been racked by financial difficulties or who had been unable to sell their farms prior to their departure, this act of kindness must have augured well for the successful establishment of the new Welsh community in Canada.

VIII

With the exception of two members of the party who contracted pneumonia, the voyage passed off without any distressing incident, and the *Orissa* berthed in Liverpool on June 10, 1902. Awaiting the Chubut Welsh on the landing stage was a group of Welshmen, the most conspicuous in his greeting being W.L.Griffith who was soon recognized by the emigrants. The Canadian agent had been tireless in his efforts to arrange a smooth transit for them. Rooms had been engaged in private boarding houses, and cabs and brakes reserved for conveying them there. What was of more immediate satisfaction to the settlers was the news that passages had been booked in the Allan liner *Numidian,* due to sail to Quebec in less than two days' time. To people desirous of reaching their new home with the minimum of delay, this information made them so exuberant as to set them apart from all other emigrants. "Taken all through they were a fine set of emigrants, Welsh in features and in temperament, Welsh in speech despite their many years' residence down South, and Welsh in their firm, set determination to push on if possible. An experienced judge remarked to me as he passed through their midst: "This lot looks likely to do something." They were all respectably dressed, and although it was evident that they had passed through hard times, there was nothing of the woebegone appearance so conspicuous amongst the foreigners. And they were all of a bunch. No one interfered with another except to help, and the presence of a blind girl standing near the bulwarks as we went aboard, whilst she formed a picture that drew forth all our sympathy, was an evidence of the spirit of community amongst them." (41)

Much time was spent in completing the formalities incident

to the sea journey to Quebec, but in the afternoon of June 11 the emigrants were invited to a luncheon officially arranged for them at the Reform Club by prominent members of the Liverpool Welsh community and of the Welsh Patagonian Committee.(42)

This was an occasion for the frank expression of feelings on many matters: regrets that Michael D. Jones's dream of a Welsh colony in Patagonia had not been realized; hopes that it would be resuscitated and brought to fulfilment in Canada; and a general appreciation that the lesson had not been lost on migratory Welshmen that loyalty to King and Empire was the prerequisite of the success of any such venture. On this last point there appeared to be unanimity amongst the Chubut Welsh. The day before, they had dispatched a message to York House in London testifying to their pleasure at finding themselves once more on British soil, and to their gratitude for the practical interest shown by the Prince of Wales in their repatriation. Now, to their gratification, W.L.Griffith read the Prince's reply to that resolution, which wished them happiness and prosperity in their Canadian home. It was followed by congratulatory telegrams, in similar language, from Chamberlain, Sir John Llewelyn, Chairman of the Welsh Patagonian Committee, and Gutyn Ebrill, the Patriarch of the colony in Patagonia. For a brief but pleasurable moment the emigrants may have felt that the wide and genuine interest taken in their fate was some compensation for the tribulations and uncertainties of the past.

On the morning of their departure, June 12, many of them attended a farewell Communion service in St. David's Welsh church. They and the rest of the party were then conveyed in waggonettes to the Alexandra Dock where the *Numidian* was berthed. Griffith had exerted his utmost endeavours to provide them with all possible comfort for the voyage. "A visit to the the *Numidian* showed that special and satisfactory arrangements had been made by the Allan Company for the reasonable comfort and convenience of the passengers. A large portion of the steerage of the vessel had been set apart as the

Welsh quarter. Spacious six and four berth rooms had been specially constructed and lighted with electricity, while special bulkheads afforded to the party complete seclusion as regards sleeping and eating accommodation from the rest of the passengers. The thoughtfulness of this arrangement was greatly appreciated, and the colonists looked forward to quite a pleasant eight or nine days' trip across the Atlantic." (43)

Despite the showery weather the scene at the dock side was colourful for between 800 and 900 emigrants, British and foreign - some of the latter in their native costumes, were awaiting the order to embark. "The Patagonian Welshman has acquired something of the swarthy Spaniard-like appearance, but retained his Welsh cheeriness and homeliness of behaviour, and these characteristics were a strong contrast to the sallow complexion and sullen proceedings of his German and Scandinavian fellow-passengers."(44)

Soon after midday the crowds swarmed up the gangways, and the Chubut party "found their quarters without difficulty, and in another hour's time might be seen seated together as one big family enjoying a good, substantial dinner." A few final and emotional adieus took place on board the vessel, for there had been an extraordinary rush of kinsfolk and friends from all parts of the Principality to greet the emigrants. Then, "at half past four the *Numidian* steamed down the river westward bound, followed by a train of ardent good wishes from every heart that beats in sympathy with those who have known how to bear misfortune bravely and to face the unknown future with hope and courage."(45)

IX

Meanwhile the advance party of settlers had not been inactive. They arrived in Winnipeg in April, and in accordance with its previous undertaking the Canadian Government afforded them every facility to choose a locality that would, in their opinion, meet with the desire of the main body of emigrants. At its request the Canadian Pacific Railway provided free transport for the leaders of the party to travel wherever they wished, and placed an experienced guide at their disposal. They first explored the territory to the north and south of Grenfell in Assiniboia, but were not particularly impressed with what they saw. Returning to Winnipeg they were invited to inspect the district to the south-west of Saltcoats, which had been acquired by the Canadian Pacific Railway. It was only after considerable deliberation and weighing of evidence that a verdict was reached in favour of this area. No pressure was exerted on the settlers from any interested quarter. It was their spontaneous choice, (46) although the fact that a former Chubut colonist, Evan Jenkins, had settled in the vicinity of Saltcoats as far back as 1892 and was making a prosperous living there, may have influenced their decision. (47)

The district and town of Saltcoats which lie about 268 miles to the north-west of Winnipeg, had been the scene of many colonizing experiments in the past.(48) Originally it had been called Stirling by the Scottish settlers who had been the first to establish themselves in the neighbourhood. When, in 1888, the Manitoba and North-Western Railway Company constructed a line through the district, the name was changed to Saltcoats to commemorate the birthplace in Scotland of the President of the Company. (49) Since then this Company had been taken over by the Canadian Pacific Railway, which was most energetic in placing emigrants along its rapidly expanding lines throughout the North-West Territories.

The district of Saltcoats had every appearance of possessing a fertile soil, adaptable for arable, pastoral or mixed farming. Yields of wheat and oats had been known to reach 80 to 90 bushels an acre, the cultivation of vegetables was equally successful, and the abundance of grasses and hay guaranteed ample fodder for livestock despite occasional droughts. The Welsh emigrants could, perhaps, not have alighted on a more favourable locality to rebuild their lives. The fact that thousands of Americans were being attracted to this and adjacent areas showed that they had chosen an opportune time to take part in the preliminary exploitation of the rich natural resources of the North-West Territories.

At midnight, June 27-28, 1902, the main party of the Chubut emigrants reached Saltcoats. Led by the Anglican medical missionary, Dr. D.G.Davies, who had accompanied them from Chubut after many years' residence in Patagonia, they made their way to their new settlement some fifteen miles from the town. Here the Canadian Government had provided an ample choice of homesteads of 160 acres, and the Immigration Agent of Winnipeg was present to assist in the allocation of holdings. The authorities had supplied tents to accommodate the newcomers until they had erected their own homes, and with the constancy and determination shown by their people in Patagonia the settlers applied themselves to "establishing a colony unique in the multi-racial settlement story of the North American continent."(50)

Difficulties, of course, were bound to arise, and in the majority of cases they originated in the precarious financial position of the settlers. It would appear that the Canadian Government had assumed that the emigrants would have sufficient funds to meet the initial costs of the settlement. This was not the case, for many families had sold their properties in Chubut for a fraction of their value, and had been further crippled by the expenses of a long journey. Although the authorities were well disposed towards the Welsh, they were reluctant to make concessions withheld from other groups of emigrants, especially as the Government had already made a payment to the Patagonian Emigration Committee in London. Requests for loans and bonus payments were therefore passed over, and the most that the Government was prepared to do was to dispatch provisions to relieve the more necessitous members of the community, and assist others to find employment whereby some Welsh girls were able to secure work in Winnipeg.(51)

But it was not all a question of money. There also seems to have been some confusion regarding the actual site of the homesteads reserved by the Government for the emigrants. This produced a most discouraging effect upon, at least, one colonist, who returned to Wales from Saltcoats in a critical frame of mind. "I have just received a visit from one of the leaders of the party that went to Canada. He has returned thoroughly convinced that the attempt is foredoomed to failure. He quotes to me Mr. Secretary Chamberlain's warning about the winter, but says that the winter is not the worst. It appears that the efforts of the Canadian Emigration Department ended with the despatch of the two agents (Griffith and Rees). When the party arrived in Saltcoats, the land they were to settle on could not be found, and it was not till two months afterwards that a proper Government surveyor came up to look for it. They had been brought there upon the map of a survey made twenty years ago, every peg and mark of which survey had disappeared. That perhaps would have mattered less but for the fact that three fourths of the sections in each township belonged by law to either the Railway Company, the Hudson Bay Company or the Schools Department, and these sections were likewise unmarked. One thing they did find however, viz the ruined cabins of a colony which had already abandoned the district convinced of its unsuitability. And now they are again looking for South Africa as their only resort."(52)

Whatever the truth of these allegations, the suggestion in

the final sentence was completely divorced from reality, for by the autumn of 1902 the colony had assumed the characteristic features of a prairie settlement of the early twentieth century. The wealthier section of the community had their log dwellings which stood out in contrast with the sod houses of their neighbours, the typical homes of relatively poor immigrants, skilfully plastered and whitewashed and built to withstand the rigours of the Canadian winter. Wells had been dug here and there, and the land around broken for the new crop.

Now that the Chubut Welsh were contented with their choice of territory and intended to reside permanently on it, the next step was to select a distinctive name for the new settlement. It was a natural thing for them to wish to acknowledge the kindness and assistance given them by their countrymen in Wales. Their inclinations in this respect may have been produed by the concurrent interest taken in the subject by one very vocal member of the Patagonian Emigration Committee, who was a personality of some repute in the Principality. The Reverend J. Ll. Thomas, better known to his contemporaries as the Vicar of Aberpergwm, opined that the historical association of the colony with Wales deserved to be perpetuated, at least in its name, since the passage of time was likely to obliterate its Welsh complexion. If a name was desirable then "I do not think a more appropriate one could be found than that of the chairman of the Committee (Sir John Llewelyn) that has promoted this "trek". It will commend itself to the pioneers as a distinctively Welsh name, as the name of their last native Prince, and, moreover, as the name of one who has prominently identified himself with the movement for their settlement in Canada . . . Only I should hope that if the name Llewelyn should be adopted, and if a prefix or suffix should be deemed necessary, it would be Tre-Llewelyn and not Llewelyn-ville after the objectionable practice of adopting place-names so prevalent in the States."(53)

The *Western Mail,* which had unreservedly supported the emigration movement to Canada, heartily approved of the suggestion, but detected a slight grammatical error in the form

CALL FROM CANADA   95

of the name as proposed by the Vicar of Aberpergwm. "As Mr.
Thomas is aware the name Llewelyn in such a connection
acquires an adjectival character, and the initial consonant is in
what grammarians call the "middle form"; hence the proper
form would be Tre Lewelyn like Tre Ddafydd, Tre Ddewi . . .
Tre Lewelyn is not only the more correct form, but more
pronounceable, and a French or an English Canadian will be in
no danger of splitting his tongue in a desperate effort to
overcome the "gander" sound."(54)

Thousands of miles to the west the Welsh settlers in their
wisdom obviated academic censure and linguistic difficulties
alike by adopting the straightforward form of Llywelyn.
Within a year or so two other townships were formed and
called Glyndwr and St. David's respectively, and from 1904
onwards the colony enjoyed uninterrupted good fortune. The
construction of a Canadian Pacific Railway line about six
miles south of the settlement improved the prospects of better
marketing arrangements for the disposal of local produce. The
decision three years later to run the Grand Trunk Pacific line
through the centre of the colony further stimulated its
economy, and led to the establishment of the village of Bangor
as the focal point of its growing commercial activities.

A price had to be paid for these material blessings, and with
few exceptions the settlers gradually succumbed to the
inexorable assimilative pressures of the society in which they
had chosen to live. The original hope of preserving their
homogeneity as a Welsh settlement, and in particular their
language, soon faded. It was not entirely their fault. No
emigrants followed in their wake from Chubut to Saltcoats,
and, in any case, by the end of 1903 all available homesteads in
the district had been taken up by other groups of settlers. To
live in isolation may have appealed to some of the oldest
amongst them, but was unacceptable to the younger
generation. Welsh is no longer spoken by the descendants of
the colonists of 1902, but the awareness of their origin has
never been effaced. "The Patagonian Welsh became part of the
Western Canadian mosaic, but they made their chief

contribution to the nation as successful farmers and builders of a community cherishing the values of their nationality in family tradition and outlook, and not in the form of exclusive and intransigent assertions of national identity."(55)

PART 3

South African vision

I

Throughout the negotiations and final arrangements for the removal of the settlers to Canada, those amongst the Chubut Welsh who favoured emigration to South Africa had continued quietly to formulate their plans. If they had attended the meetings organized by W.L. Griffith and W.J.Rees during their mission to Patagonia, they had remained impervious to their arguments, although it would seem that their opposition to settling in Canada was partly a deep-seated distrust of the climate there. For the moment, however, there was no immediate prospect of emigrating to South Africa because of the unexpected prolongation of the Boer War by the guerilla tactics of the Boer commandos. It was only after the latter had been reduced to submission and the territories of the Transvaal and the Orange River Colony securely occupied by the British army, that any constructive colonization policy could be prosecuted in South Africa.

Until that happened the pro-South African party in Chubut had to wait upon events. But it rightly judged that nothing could better promote its objectives than the establishment of contacts with the influential circles which were known to be closely associated with the political and industrial development of South Africa as an appanage of the British Empire. To present themselves as experienced colonists who had survived extreme tests of endurance, was likely to recommend them to powerful interests which had an eye for the economic potentialities of unexploited lands, and were looking for the right type of settlers to work them permanently and profitably.

No less important was the evidence that they could produce of their loyalty to the Crown, their attachment to British traditions, and their desire to place their energies at the disposal of the British Government instead of wasting them in an alien land. On this score the Chubut Welsh were in a strong position. Not only had they shown much reluctance to accept Argentine nationality, but as far as South Africa was concerned they were, for the most part, anti-Boer in sentiment. It was said that a number of young men in the valley would have joined the British forces as volunteer scouts if circumstances had permitted. At a time when the British Government regarded the establishment of British institutions and way of life in newly acquired territories as being no less desirable than the planting of seed, the pro-South African emigration group in Chubut felt that they could present their case with some confidence.

The first step was to win the ear of the man who was convinced that he possessed the capacity and the will to make Britain the paramount power in Africa from the Cape to Cairo. From the day of his arrival at Cape Town, Cecil Rhodes had conducted an unremitting campaign against the multifarious commercial and political interests which opposed and obstructed his ambition. In 1889 the British South Africa Company, the spear point of his unbounded Imperialist designs received its charter of incorporation which virtually gave it a free hand to extend its control over native territory to the north and west of the then independent Boer colonies of the Orange River Republic and the Transvaal. Since that year the Company had steadily widened its sphere of influence and activity, obtaining mineral concessions from native chiefs, building railways and making grants of lands to settlers. (1) Under its powerful, almost state, patronage, the fortunes of a reliable and determined group of colonists stood a good chance of being assured.

Early in October, 1901, Rhodes received a letter from Llwyd ap Iwan, who at the time was preparing to return to Chubut after he and Benbow Phillips had failed to persuade the British Government to exercise its supposed sovereign rights over Patagonia. Llwyd may have been acting on instructions from his colleagues of the Emigration Committee at home. It is also possible that he may have been advised to enter into correspondence with Rhodes by Brynmor Jones, who was of the opinion that if the Chubut Welsh had to emigrate at all, it should be to South Africa and not to Canada. (2)

The letter could not have been better framed to appeal to Rhodes whose sympathy for British settlers under any rule but that of their own people was well known. Llwyd introduced himself as "one of a community of nearly four thousand Welsh settled in Patagonia who stand in relation to the Argentine Government in a very similar position to that of the Uitlanders (British settlers under Boer rule) in relation to the Government of the Transvaal. The only difference lies in the fact that while the British Government were under an obligation to redress the grievances of its subjects in South Africa, we Uitlanders of South America had no such grounds in the London Convention (3) under which we could hope to induce the British Government to intervene on our behalf." Having contrasted the impotence of the Chubut community with the happier situation of the British settlers in South Africa who had been rescued from their Boer governors by military intervention, Llwyd made the additional point of predicting the fate in store for the Patagonian Welsh if they were abandoned in their predicament. They would be forced to become Spaniards and adopt the Spanish language, and the paucity of suitable farming land in Patagonia would be exploited by the authorities to constrain them to renounce their British nationality.

There followed an open hint that the transfer of such a community of dedicated Britishers and experienced colonists would be a valuable acquisition to South Africa. Through their own efforts the Welsh had built "the most flourishing colony without exception in South America", and constructed hundreds of miles of irrigating canals without any capital. Moreover, "the colonists have always been ready to take up arms in the interests of peace, and on several occasions have successfully defended themselves against the raids of Indians."

In the light of the long unbroken years of amity between the Welsh and the Patagonian Indians, this was an extraordinary statement to make. Either Llwyd was referring to disputes and clashes unrecorded in the annals of the Chubut settlement, or he wished to imply that in the event of any native rising in South Africa the Patagonian Welsh would be quite capable of taking care of themselves.

"As I am returning to Patagonia in the course of this coming month," he ended his letter, "I am desirous of knowing if you consider it probable that we Chubut colonists could get a grant of suitable land in any region in South Africa, where we could settle together under the protection of the British flag." (4)

If the letter was received by Rhodes he passed it on to the Board of the South Africa Company, and it was read at its meeting on October 28, 1901. With so many other matters awaiting a decision, it might well have been relegated to the Company's files but for the effect it produced on Lyttelton Gell, one of the Directors, who was present.

For many years Gell had enjoyed the intimate friendship and confidence of Lord Milner, now Governor-General of South Africa. They had been contemporaries at Oxford, and although their paths had somewhat diverged since then, their involvement in South African affairs had reinforced the personal links between them and the similarity of their views on the prosecution of British interests there. Both men shared the conviction, which they maintained by constant correspondence, that the economic rehabilitation of, and the stability of British rule in, South Africa was conditional upon the influx of settlers of British stock. Milner himself had no doubt that the peaceful assimilation of the Boer people and their territories to-British administration depended, in the last resort, upon a judicious land settlement which would allow the infiltration of British colonists sufficiently self-reliant and experienced to make their influence felt on their poorer and more conservative Boer neighbours, both politically and economically. (5) In his own words, "On the political side I attach the greatest importance of all to the increase of the British population. . . .If ten years hence there are three men of

British race to two of Dutch, the country will be safe and prosperous. If there are three of Dutch to two of British, we shall have perpetual difficulty. The majority of the agricultural population will always be Dutch. This does not matter provided there are some strong English districts and that, in most districts, there are a sufficient number of British to hold their own." (6) These were ideas to which Gell subscribed not only with partisan fervour, but with a shrewd assessment of the advantages that would accrue to the South Africa Company if Boer militancy were defused by the presence and activities of British colonists.

Llwyd's letter had the effect of persuading Lyttelton Gell to act immediately on it, and his first concern was to obtain as much information as was available about the antecedents and conditions of the Chubut settlers. On the day that the letter was read to the Board of the South Africa Company, he wrote to the Foreign Office to explain that, at Milner's request, he was privately "beating up suitable agricultural settlers for establishment in South Africa" and wished to examine the qualifications of the Patagonian Welsh. "A generation spent in the Argentine appears to have converted them into warm Imperialists." (7) He was disposed to help them and requested copies of official reports on the colony.

These he received in due course with an intimation that the Government would be reluctant to see the Canadian emigration scheme impeded in any way, or any use made of passages in the reports which might be construed as offensive to the Argentine Government. Gell wrote again to remove any apprehensions on these points. "The rights or wrongs of the colonists' quarrels with Argentine officialdom do not affect my present object which is merely to collect materials for judging (1) whether it is worth while to make an effort to transport them either to the Orange River Colony to help Lord Milner's policy of land settlement or to Rhodesia; (2) whether the Chubut Emigration Committee can be relied upon. On the other hand, it would be a serious consideration if there was reason to believe that these colonists are still inspired by that intolerance of authority and innate craving for secession of which there have been signs in their past history." (8) It would seem that what Gell had read in the reports concerning the inflexibility of the Chubut Welsh in resisting assimilation had raised some doubts in his mind as to their future docility in political matters. He may also have remembered Llwyd ap Iwan's earnest desire that they should be allowed to settle as one community in South Africa. However, he felt that such questions could be left to the future. With the permission of the Foreign Office he arranged for copies to be made of the reports, excluding certain controversial passages, and sent them to Lord Milner and other interested circles in South Africa.

He also wrote a letter to Llwyd ap Iwan in which he asked for detailed information about Chubut. It arrived inopportunely for Llwyd who replied: "I am sorry that I am not able to answer in full your most interesting and important letter as my time is so taken up now that I am on the point of departure for Buenos Aires." (9) Llwyd added that his brother-in-law, Professor Thomas Rhys, "will be able to give you all the information about the Colony from its foundation until now," and this led to a correspondence between the two men and to Rhys's offer to assist in any scheme to further emigration to South Africa.*
"I dare say," he assured Gell, "we shall have some plan to suggest with regard to the settling of some of the Chubut colonists in South Africa." (10)

Initially the reaction in that country to the reports on the Chubut settlers was one of caution. The authorities, for the time being, were inclined to the opinion that the first offer of land should be given to those members of the British armed forces who wished to settle in the Transvaal and the Orange River Colony. Even Milner was constrained to recognize this priority, although there was little harmony between him and the military on other matters. "Chubut, to my great regret I can't take on," he wrote to Gell. "We have now so large a

* See *supra* pp. 81.

number of settlers, many of them excellent, on the spot clamouring for some definite arrangement, and we are so weather-bound and paralysed by military policy, that I should only be aggravating an already great difficulty if I brought some more eligible men out." (11) There was also the feeling that prospective settlers should be carefully selected as to their character and means, and that the British Government should discourage any notion that it was ready to dip into its pocket to provide free passages to any would-be colonists.

Gell made a note of this hesitancy to fling the doors of South Africa open to the Patagonian Welsh, but continued with his inquiries. On one particular point he was relieved of his doubts. "I have gathered from independent sources that the Canadian migration has provided a safety valve for a certain amount of restlessness." (12) On the other hand, that same migration had reduced by some hundreds the number of settlers who were determined to leave Chubut. In these circumstances, Gell thought it best to leave matters alone until a recrudescence of enthusiasm in favour of South Africa should again manifest itself. Should that occur the best solution, he thought, would be the transfer of the Welsh to Rhodesia. He was unaware, despite his investigations, that a new impetus had already been given in Chubut to the movement for emigration to South Africa.

II

The colonists were still engaged in restoring some semblance of economic order after the floods of the two previous years, when a third inundation occurred on June 10, 1902. The valley was flooded to a depth of fifteen feet in some places, and the losses and despair that followed deepened the conviction that the settlement had received its *coup de grace* leaving no alternative to its inhabitants but to abandon Chubut.

The Argentine Government again came to the aid of the afflicted colony, and once more offered the settlers the possibility of obtaining land and greater security against floods in other regions of the Republic. But the action of that Government, a month or so before the disaster, had already revived the suspicions of the Welsh regarding the motives behind the offer. On May 1, a Presidential Decree had appeared in the Government Gazette to the effect that 60 square miles of territory along the west coast of Chubut were to be set aside for colonization by Boer families. It transpired that two Boer leaders, Baumann and Ricciardi, had arrived in the Argentine and concluded an agreement with the authorities for Boer settlement. Baumann was a former burger of the Orange River Colony, and Ricciardi an Italian who had fought alongside the Boers and was said to have married a granddaughter of the late President Kruger. There was further talk that Baumann proposed to take up immediate residence on the land allotted by the Government, and that Ricciardi, who had been busily collecting money for the project in Buenos Aires, would return to Europe and bring back a number of Boer families to Patagonia. (13)

To the Argentine Government a new batch of colonists, particularly those experienced in farming, was always welcome, and their political and social antecedents were generally of little account. At this time the arrival of new settlers was eagerly awaited, for emigration to the Argentine had fallen away recently, and almost as many people were leaving the Republic as were coming in. (14) Moreover, due to the mediation of the British Government in the boundary dispute between Chile and the Argentine, and the good offices of its representative, Sir Thomas Holdich, the danger of war over conflicting claims along the Andes had receded, and the Argentine Government was keen to resume its policy of colonizing Patagonia.

To the Chubut Welsh, however, who were already battling against a growing intermixture of different nations and cultures within the narrow confines of the valley, the proposed Boer settlement was a further step in the process of the gradual strangulation of their national identity and language. And as far as the terms of the agreement between the Boer leaders and the Government were concerned, they must have noticed that the authorities showed a greater readiness to hand over title deeds to the Boers than they had ever done to the Welsh. The new Boer settlement was therefore to be made as permanent as favourable concessions could make it possible. (15) It was under the pressure of these events that the supporters of the South African emigration movement decided on their next move. This time it was not to be a tentative negotiation with any particular company whose interests lay in that undeveloped country, but a direct approach to the British Government itself.

The initial step was taken by two members of the colony, W. M. Hughes and John G. Jones, who wrote personally to Chamberlain. The Colonial Secretary was assured of a general desire in Chubut to move to South Africa, and of the preference of the settlers for the Transvaal or the Orange River Colony as regions where they would enjoy a climate similar to that in Patagonia, and could make practical use of their experience over the years in irrigation. The Colonial Secretary was requested to advise them whether an area of land, some

200-300 square miles, could be reserved exclusively for a Welsh colony, and whether the British Government would assist in the transfer of colonists and live stock (with some farming implements) from Port Madryn to South Africa. He was asked to state the terms on which land could be made available for intending emigrants; and, finally, there was a suggestion that delegates from Chubut were ready to travel to South Africa to view the land offered, if they could be provided with free passage. (16)

These letters did not reach Chamberlain until August, but when he read them they confirmed the impression he had received from other quarters that, given the opportunity, there would be an impressive emigration of Chubut Welshmen(17), who had again demonstrated their loyalty to the Crown by assembling at Trelew on June 26, under the chairmanship of the "Archdruid" of Chubut, to celebrate the coronation of Edward VII. (18)

But there were other considerations which could not be ignored. The previous year, when Lord Milner was in England, he and Chamberlain had touched on the matter of emigration from Chubut to South Africa, but nothing positive had been envisaged. Since then Milner had urged caution and discretion in sending colonists of any kind unless they were specifically requested by him. (19) Nevertheless a directive by the Colonial Secretary showed that he was not unsympathetic to the messages contained in the letters from the two Chubut colonists. "The occurrence of a third serious flood. . . .is bringing the emigration question to the fore again. Mr. Hughes proposes South Africa, and a delegation to visit it. Send copy of this to Foreign Office, and ask them to inform Mr Hughes through Minister (at Buenos Aires) that no statement can be made at present as to assistance, but that if the colonists like to send delegates to S. Africa, they will be given indulgence passages from this country (through which I presume that they must pass), and Lord Milner will be asked to provide them with free passes on the Central South Africa Railways, and provide other facilities to enable them to see the country . . . .And send the correspondence to Lord Milner with some of the earlier reports and Bluebook about Chubut to show him what sort of people they are." (20)

A fortnight later the Colonial Secretary received another letter. It was dated from Llanuwchllyn in Merionethshire, and the writer had signed himself A.O. Vaughan.

III

Captain Arthur Owen Vaughan, later to be better known in Wales as Owen Rhoscomyl, author and dramatist, had left his home in the Clwyd valley at an early age in search of adventure. (21) He had wandered for many years over the face of the globe, and the outbreak of hostilities in South Africa had brought him, like many other Welshmen, to that country. He had enlisted in Rimington's Rifles, one of the irregular companies of horse which had fought against the Boers and given a good account of themselves. He had later transferred to the Canadian Scouts and been promoted to the rank of senior squadron leader.

According to his own account of events Vaughan was with his regiment at Heilbron when peace was proclaimed. Aware that his military services would no longer be required, he was casting about for some other employment when he received a letter from the Cambrian Society in Capetown. This informed him that the Society, whose President was Mr. W. Thorpe, the Mayor of Capetown, had made representations to Sir Gordon Spriggs, the Cape Prime Minister, for the transfer of the Chubut Welsh to South Africa, and had requested that their appeal should be communicated to Lord Milner. Milner had considered their request and had returned a favourable answer.(22) Moreover, he had proposed that the Society should send a delegate to Johannesburg, where the preliminaries to the transfer could be thoroughly discussed, and a concerted plan agreed upon by the delegate and the British authorities for expediting the passage of the colonists. The letter ended with an invitation to Vaughan to act as the Society's delegate, and although there were apparently better prospects in other directions, he agreed to accept the office.(23)

Shortly after, the Canadian Scouts were ordered to Pretoria to be disbanded, and Vaughan took advantage of this to contact the British administration in that town. Lord Milner was absent on business in Johannesburg, and arrangements were made for Vaughan to meet his chief private secretary, Mr. Walrond. The meeting was formal but friendly, and Walrond explained that the whole matter of a Welsh settlement had been entrusted to Mr. John Buchan.*

Buchan had arrived in South Africa in 1901 as secretary to Lord Milner, and for the past year he had been expending his time and energy in devising solutions for the twin problems of resettling Boer soldiers and prisoners of war on their farms and finding suitable land for importunate British settlers.(24) His experiences and his awareness of the opposing interests of Boers and British had led him to one firm conclusion, that the ultimate goal of land settlement should be the fusion of the two peoples and the gradual erosion of mutual suspicions and racial antagonism. This could only be achieved by infiltrating colonists of British stock into the rural areas, and selecting such as would remain loyal to British traditions and way of life, but who would also induce their Boer neighbours in time to cooperate in a policy of advancing the interests of all classes of the community. "An influx of such a class would consolidate South African sentiment, and when self-government comes, protect imperial interests better than any constitutional guarantee." (25)

Vaughan's interview with Buchan was an immediate success. The two men found no difficulty in reaching an agreement on many points. To Vaughan's gratification Buchan undertook to reserve for the Chubut Welsh an area known as Magatoland in the Zoutpansberg in northern Transvaal. He also promised the most favourable conditions for their settlement. Vaughan communicated the results of the meeting to the Cambrian Society in Capetown, who approved of them and asked him to be responsible for implementing the scheme.

A second meeting with Buchan followed, but on this occasion there arose a serious misunderstanding, of which the

* later Lord Tweedsmuir, author and historian.

two were perhaps not aware at the time, but which was to have unpleasant repercussions. When Vaughan brought up the question of appointing an agent to see the scheme through, Buchan explained that since the Colonial Office was the department primarily concerned with any policy of settlement in Crown lands, the selection of any such official rested in the hands of the Colonial Secretary. He advised Vaughan to proceed without delay to London. "Go now and get yourself appointed," he is reported to have told him, "and we will get the work going at once, the quicker the better." (26)

Vaughan may have read more into these words than Buchan had intended. However, encouraged by the latter's reception and collaboration, he made his way to Capetown and there met the President and members of the Cambrian Society. In order to save time it was decided to cable the Welsh Patagonian Committee in London, and urge them to intervene with the Colonial Secretary for Vaughan's appointment as agent and its official confirmation by telegraph. No acknowledgment of the cable was received and Vaughan, recollecting Buchan's advice, proceeded to London without further delay. There he discovered that the Welsh Patagonian Committee no longer existed, and came to the conclusion that if the plan for a Welsh colony in South Africa was to be pushed through, he would have to rely on his own initiative and efforts.

He first consulted a former member of the Committee, Brynmor Jones, who was sufficiently impressed by Vaughan's arguments to provide him with a letter of introduction to the Colonial Office. "Though I have not the slightest reason to doubt Captain Vaughan's representations, I am naturally not in a position to verify any of the facts as to the proposal which he has laid before me. But I think he should have a chance of being heard by your office." (27)

Vaughan was received by the Colonial Office that same day, and was afforded every opportunity to elaborate the scheme which he had in mind for the Chubut Welsh. In return he was requested to sound the opinion of people in Wales who might be interested in it, and to draw up a memorandum for the consideration of the Colonial Office. During the four weeks that he spent in the Principality he was able to meet and interrogate a number of Patagonian Welsh and others, and incorporated their views and his own proposals in the memorandum which he forwarded to the Colonial Office. At the same time he entered into correspondence with Chubut, urging the colonists to confer together on the matter of emigration and to appoint committees, one of which should go to South Africa to view the country, and the other act on behalf of those who wished to emigrate. Deeming it expedient to acquaint the Colonial Secretary with the reasons that had brought him all the way from Pretoria to Britain, and in the hope that his services would be appreciated, he wrote the letter from Llanuwchllyn which Chamberlain received in due course.

IV

Whatever effect Vaughan hoped to produce by his letter, Chamberlain regarded it primarily as evidence that matters were progressing more rapidly in South Africa than he had anticipated, and that it was time for the Colonial Office to take them in hand and guide the projected Chubut emigration along practical and desirable lines. It was essential, in the first place, to coordinate the views of the British Government and the administration in Johannesburg on the entire question of emigration, and persuade the latter to be advised on matters of detail by the Colonial Office. In a letter to Lord Milner, Chamberlain repeated his offer of free passages for Chubut delegates to visit South Africa if Milner could arrange for gratuitous travelling facilities on the South African railways. But he emphasized two points: that the Chubut settlers should be informed of the precise terms of their removal and settlement, and that a prior decision would have to be taken as to whether the cost of their transfer from the Argentine was to be borne by Government funds. On one other aspect of the emigration, which Vaughan had raised in his letter, the Colonial Secretary was not prepared to make concessions. "I fear that it will be found impossible to arrange for the settlers to take with them their wagons and other heavy stock as suggested in Captain Vaughan's letter, and I think it not improbable that when this fact is pointed out to them, many who may have been contemplating emigration may decide not to leave Chubut." He added that he would await Milner's observations before proceeding any further. (28)

It was, in fact, the Chubut settlers who forced the pace in these somewhat protracted proceedings. On September 3, a telegram arrived at the Colonial Office which read: "Will

Government defray expenses three delegates. Africa Apiwan."
To the officials who racked their brains in trying to decipher
the signature, it was completely incomprehensible. A
meticulous examination of the list of institutions in the
London Directory proved unavailing, and the telegram might
have been passed over if it had not been discovered by chance
that it had some connection with the Chubut emigration
scheme. (29) The urgency of the message was appreciated, and
the British Minister in Buenos Aires was immediately directed
to inform Llwyd ap Iwan that the Government had every
intention of granting indulgence passages to South Africa.
Later, a letter from Lord Milner confirmed that he, for his part,
accepted the obligation of paying the expenses of the Chubut
delegates in South Africa. (30)

A more comprehensive memorandum reached Chamberlain
from the South African Emigration Committee about the same
time. It was forwarded through the British Legation in Buenos
Aires in order, it would seem, to avoid rousing the suspicions of
the Argentine officials in Chubut. (31) The memorial was to the
effect that the Emigration Committee had been set up after a
public meeting in Gaiman on August 30, with D. S. Jones,
formerly of Rhymni, as chairman and Llwyd ap Iwan as secretary. It outlined the circumstances which had driven many
colonists to the conclusion that the only feasible solution to
their difficulties lay in emigration, and repeated the enquiries
about the conditions of settlement in South Africa. Its last
paragraph expressed a sentiment which Chamberlain could be
expected to applaud. "The deepest satisfaction is felt by the
whole community at the successful termination of the war, and
there is a loyal and fervent belief in the prosperous and peaceful
future of South Africa finally united under the British flag."
(32) Since arrangements had been made to expedite the
passage of the Chubut delegates to South Africa, the Colonial
Office interpreted the memorial as a reaffirmation of the
wishes of the Patagonian Welsh, and settled down in the
reassuring belief that the emigration plan had every chance of
getting off the ground.

It was at this juncture that Captain Vaughan reappeared on the scene and in a rather militant mood. He had not relaxed his activities since the compilation of his memorandum to the Colonial Office. He had interested himself in the problem of finding the cheapest and quickest sea route from Chubut, and had put forward the suggestion that one of the cattle boats running between Buenos Aires and Capetown would provide the best service in this respect. (33) But he had received no intimation of what status the Colonial Office was prepared to grant him in all these negotiations, and whether, in fact, he would be regarded as other than a useful liaison in a common cause. His anxiety had not been laid to rest by the knowledge that messages had been transmitted by the Colonial Office to Chubut without his being notified of them, and it was the ambiguity of his situation that determined him to seek another interview with the Colonial Office. "I am compelled to beg of you," he wrote, "to kindly let me know just where I stand now. Am I to cut the loss of some hundreds spent, of good billets lost, and turn now elsewhere to look for work if I can get it?" (34) And he referred in no uncertain terms to his expectation that, consequent upon his exchange of views with John Buchan, he would be employed and paid for his work by the British Government.

It was a statement which took the Colonial Office by surprise. Looking up their correspondence with Lord Milner, they found nothing in writing to corroborate that Vaughan had been in close touch with the British administration in South Africa, or that the latter had led him to assume that he would receive an appointment in any way associated with the settlement of the Patagonian Welsh in South Africa. Official reaction displayed an understandable annoyance, and both the British administration in Johannesburg and John Buchan came in for some criticism. "If Mr. Buchan really advised Captain Vaughan as stated, his advice was very bad, for if they want him at all they want him in South Africa not in England, and could easily have proposed to give him the job of superintending the settlement by despatch. It seems to me that it would be a mistake to appoint an officer to superintend the settlement until we know (a) the result of the negotiation with the delegates and (b) what number of settlers really do intend to leave Chubut and go to South Africa." (35)

A second visit by Vaughan to the Colonial Office on September 28 did not do much to stabilize his position. But, to his credit, this did not dispose him to wash his hands of the emigration scheme. On the contrary, he found time that same day to write to the department and submit further proposals, one of which in particular showed that he was conversant with the more complex economic and financial aspects of colonization. "My own notion was, as stated, that the Colonial Office here would advance the necessary capital sum to transport these people and their stock on a commercial basis, as could easily be done, and that the proportionate debt incurred by each settler would be a first charge on his holding and stock in South Africa. Or the debt might be handed over to Lord Milner to be added to the sum total of indebtedness for land, seeds, buildings, etc, when he took possession of his holding in Magatoland. When I left Pretoria there was no question of bringing over these people's stock, for the reason that no one knew what ideally good stock for South Africa it really was. By transferring that stock with them, however, you land them as prosperous men able to carry and pay off a stiff indebtedness instead of as beggars beginning anew with nothing but debts and no assets save time and labour. Pretoria is working at more schemes than one to restock S. Africa. Here is a scheme killing two birds with one stone, settlers and stock together." (36)

It appeared a sound enough proposition, although it ran counter to Chamberlain's decision that no live stock was to be transported from Chubut to South Africa. But it was doomed never to be discussed because of other developments which affected Vaughan personally. A telegram to Milner enquiring about his services and whether they were indispensable, was almost brusque in tone. "What are the facts? Are his services required, if so on what terms? (37) Milner's reply made it abundantly clear that Vaughan had not been promised any employment by the South African administration, but had merely been advised to consult the Colonial Office as to the possibility of a post as agent. And Milner pointed out that, in any case, it was for the Chubut Welsh themselves to decide whether Vaughan was the right person to promote their interests in that capacity. (38) In a further communication, which showed that he had evidently reconsidered the matter, Milner supplied the additional information that Vaughan had been told of the intention of the Transvaal Government to pay a reasonable salary to any nominee of the Chubut settlers who took charge of the actual work of transporting them to South Africa. It was appreciated that Vaughan had devoted time and energy to the scheme, and possessed the requisite ability and drive to implement it. But Milner insisted once again that "it would be clearly impossible for the (Transvaal) Government to invite settlers from another country, and then force upon them a representative to act for them" (39) In the light of Milner's exposition of what appeared to be Vaughan's precipitancy in the matter, the Colonial Office felt that there was no alternative but to inform the latter that there was no vacancy for an agent, and that he would be considered if one should arise.

It is not difficult to imagine Vaughan's disappointment, but in the meantime he had received news from South Africa which added a good measure of resentment to his mortification. During his absence in England, a certain J. A. Evans had insinuated himself into the counsels of the land settlement officials in the Transvaal, and had succeeded, to all intents and purposes, in supplanting Vaughan. A copy of a letter from Evans to the Mayor of Capetown made it painfully evident to Vaughan that all the efforts he had made to arrive at the initial agreement with John Buchan were being capitalized by the newcomer. He was particularly exasperated by Evans's suggestion that the Chubut Welsh should be settled in Basutoland rather than Magatoland, contrary to the original decision. But what cut him to the quick was the final passage in Evans's letter, which seemed to indicate that he had been completely forgotten by the British officials in Pretoria. "The Private

Secretary (Walrond) and Mr. Buchan, Head of the Agriculture Staff, asked me if I would go up to Magatoland, but I thought it better to wait until the (Chubut) delegates come. I told them I should be pleased if they would put me in something to wait and they promised me they would."(40)

In a letter to the Colonial Office which scarcely concealed his bitterness, Vaughan enclosed Evans's communication and commented: "It explains itself pretty clearly, and incidentally its final sentence shows that appointments are going on in connection with the emigration of a portion of the Welsh settlers in Chubut to South Africa. But I had no intention of meddling with anything less than the whole of those settlers, as my letters and assurances from Chubut implied to be possible, nay to be determined upon. The point in the whole thing which I look at is the easy way in which Mr Buchan sends me off to London to get an appointment, and then sets the first comer into my place after I have set things going. It is most instructive to me, and doubtless some day may be entertaining, even useful perhaps, now that I have to find something to do." (41)

The Colonial Office thought that it was "rather a rude letter", but that, nevertheless, Vaughan had a substantial grievance. However, the department was never called upon to remedy it. Captain Vaughan had ventilated his feelings, and that was about all he could do in the circumstances. Being accustomed to the vagaries of fortune, he quickly turned his attention to other employment. If he had failed to have a hand in the establishment of a Welsh colony in South Africa, at least his knowledge of that country and its people gave him a further footing in the literary world into which he had already penetrated with the publication of some novels. Two years later a volume of Afrikans stories, entitled *Old Henrik's Tales,* was published in London under his name.(42)

V

Meanwhile the South African Emigration Committee in Chubut had been galvanized into activity by messages from Clarke, the British Chargé d'Affaires in Buenos Aires, that their proposal to send delegates to South Africa had been accepted in London and approved of in Johannesburg. A letter from Captain Vaughan had also raised their hopes tremendously, for he had written "giving a most favourable account of the land in the north of Transvaal which, he affirms, it is proposed to set aside for the Welsh colonists of Chubut. He also dwells on the easy terms on which the land will be granted and on the facilities to be afforded by the Government in the way of supplying seed, implements, stock and all needful materials at cost price to the settlers." (43)

At a meeting of the Committee in Gaiman, the decision was taken to select three delegates to travel to the Transvaal and to view and report on the territory reserved for a Welsh colony. The choice fell on Llwyd ap Iwan, D.S.Jones and R.J. Roberts. The problem was, of course, to raise enough money to cover the costs of their journey, and commenting on this dilemma, brought to his notice by Llwyd ap Iwan, Clarke wrote to the Foreign Office that "the men selected are, if I am rightly informed, possessed of but small, private means, and the distress in Chubut, owing to the floods of the last few years, is such that funds for the purpose of supplying the delegates with money could not easily be raised among the colonists themselves." (44) However, anxieties on this score were relieved by assurances from the Colonial Office and Lord Milner that all travelling and subsistence expenses would be defrayed officially.

It had been intended that the delegates should travel to

South Africa *via* England, but this was later rejected in favour of the cheapest and most direct route from Buenos Aires to Capetown. All arrangements having been satisfactorily concluded, the three delegates arrived in the Argentine capital by November 20. But bearing in mind the rather exuberant prospects which Vaughan had predicted in his letter to Llwyd ap Iwan, the Colonial Office had again insisted in a letter to Lord Milner that "it will be necessary to arrive at a clear understanding not only as to the terms upon which land is to be assigned to the settlers in South Africa, but also as to the arrangements to be made for their departure from Chubut, the amount of stock which they may be permitted to take with them, etc." (45)

The delegates left Buenos Aires on November 20 on board the *Langton Grange,* which was due to dock in Durban eighteen days or so later. They did not have sufficient money to pay for their passages, and the expenses were accordingly met by the British Legation. From Durban they travelled by train to the Transvaal, and as soon as their arrival was notified to the Government, steps were taken for them to visit all land open to settlement, and to enter into discussions on their choice of territory.

They were no less careful and searching in their inquiries and investigations than the advance party of the Chubut emigrants to Canada. By April they were in a position to enter into negotiations with the authorities, and the two sides met in Pretoria. It emerged from the discussions that the delegates had chosen the district of Christiana as the most promising region for a Welsh community, and that the Transvaal authorities had agreed to their choice.

At first sight it might have seemed surprising that the delegates should have selected this particular district. Christiana lay in the south-western corner of the Transvaal with the Orange River Colony, Cape Colony and Bechuanaland as its immediate neighbours. The country around was high veldt suitable for raising stock, but it suffered severely from dry seasons; so much so that although the Vaal river flowed steadily through the district the tributaries of that river dried up completely at intervals. Christiana had never been able to maintain itself on locally grown crops. Grain, as well as fuel, had to be regularly imported, and the absence of a railway added appreciably to the price of both commodities besides limiting contacts with the outside world. However, as opposed to these drawbacks, it was generally recognized that a well planned system of irrigation would reverse the situation, and transform Christiana into a highly productive and prosperous region.

The demands made by any scheme of irrigation on human ingenuity and labour were not likely to daunt the Welsh delegates. What had been achieved by their countrymen in this respect in Patagonia, and in far worse conditions, could be repeated in South Africa if necessary. But it seemed highly likely that it would not be necessary. Llwyd ap Iwan and his two colleagues must have known of the Transvaal Government's intention to embark on an irrigation scheme at Christiana. This was the construction of a canal or furrow along the bank of the Vaal, which would draw off enough water to irrigate the land in the vicinity and extend the area of cultivation. (46) Eventually it was hoped to obtain the cooperation of the Governments of Cape Colony and the Orange River Colony to build a dam across the Vaal above Christiana and thereby secure a sufficient storage of water to irrigate 45,000 acres of fertile but parched land. (47) But, for the moment, the Welsh delegates could plausibly argue that an area, where the Transvaal authorities were ready to commit themselves to supply even a moderate amount of water, was the obvious and desirable place to settle the Chubut emigrants, despite the fact that certain defects had not escaped their notice.

Following upon the meeting in Pretoria the Government put forward a number of proposals which it hoped would be acceptable to the three Welshmen. The letter which contained them suggested that they should at least form a basis for discussion.

"It is proposed that the Settler shall receive a holding of fifty acres of irrigable land and five acres of dry land at a valuation which with a moderate rate of interest and sinking fund would cover the cost of the land and works to the Government. The rates of interest and amortization viz 4% and 1¾% per annum respectively as provided in the Settlers' Ordinance should be adhered to. When the holdings have been purchased, freehold title would of course be given to the Settler.

Until the control of the running waters in the Transvaal Colony is secured in the public interest to the Government, a sufficient supply of water cannot be guaranteed, but, as you are aware, legislation is contemplated which would remove this difficulty....No effort would be spared to advance the interests and welfare of the settlers in every possible way. The Government, is prepared.....to offer you on behalf of those you represent the first choice of any of the irrigation settlements which may be laid out in this colony either on the Vaal river or elsewhere, on the understanding that such option shall be exercised within three months."*

It was suggested, at the end of the letter, that since Llwyd ap Iwan had announced his intention to remain for some time in the colony, he should be appointed as agent to transmit any further communications from Chubut to the Government.(48)

The delegates found little to commend itself in the proposals, just as, judging by one passage in their reply, they had discovered much in the Transvaal that was not to their liking. "Our experience of live stock and the knowledge we have gained of this country with its many risks to the farmer in the way of locust visitation, hail storms, horse and cattle sickness, etc, and the many difficulties and drawbacks that have to be encountered at the outset of any such enterprise as the present one" confirmed their opinion that the financial terms were unacceptable. Moreover, their long years of intensive experiments with irrigation had enabled them to detect certain fundamental weaknesses in the projected water scheme at Christiana.

* This communication was dated April 24, 1903.

"We consider that a preferent right should be granted in respect of a certain quantity of water over a certain portion (say one-third) of the area of irrigable land, thus securing the settler against the monopolizing of the water by a future settlement or organization formed for irrigation purposes higher up the stream. In support of this we would draw your attention to the present supply of water in the Vaal river. The volume of water running in the bed of the river at Christiana at the time of our recent visit would not amount to double the quantity necessary to supply an area to be irrigated of equal extent to the one under consideration. As no rains may be expected before September or October, which will materially affect the volume of water in the Vaal, it is obvious that the supply during the seasons it is most needed will be insufficient." As to the proposed canal or furrow to be built by the Government: "In connection with this, it is our duty to point out that as the projected canal for a long distance will be located along a bed of limestone, it is quite possible that a large quantity, if not all, of the water may be absorbed before it reaches the settler. The danger also of percolation from the canal should be borne in mind." Finally, the delegates expressed the wish " to be allowed to suggest that the question of transporting settlers, their stock, agricultural implements, etc, from Patagonia to the Transvaal be postponed for future consideration." (49)

It was a disappointing conclusion to long months of patient preparation, constant travelling and negotiations which had begun on a high note of optimism. Nevertheless, there was no suggestion or inclination on either side to abandon the emigration scheme. Proposals and counter-proposals were regarded as amenable to adjustment, and the idea warmly welcomed that Llwyd ap Iwan should stay in Pretoria to keep in close touch with the authorities. In fact, such was the expectation of both parties that the final outcome would be an arrangement satisfactory to all concerned, that D.S.Jones and R.J.Roberts felt themselves able to assure Lord Milner that fifty families would be ready to leave Chubut for the Transvaal in two months. (50) The two delegates began their return journey from Pretoria towards the end of April, and were back in Buenos Aires by June 3. Here Roberts fell ill and had to spend some time in the British Hospital there before he and Jones could take the steamer to Chubut to report to the South African Emigration Committee. (51)

VI

They arrived home to be informed of two discouraging developments. The first was that, owing to an outbreak of foot and mouth disease, the exportation or transport of cattle from the Argentine was strictly forbidden. To convey live stock from Port Madryn would constitute a breach of the law, although the prohibition was later modified to the extent of permitting cattle to be shipped to those countries prepared to receive Argentine live stock.(52) Whether South Africa would show willingness in this respect remained to be seen.

The other piece of information was more serious. It was a message from Lord Milner that certain difficulties had arisen over the distribution of water from the Vaal river, due to the inability of the Governments of the Transvaal and Cape Colony to see eye to eye on the matter. This was tantamount to a warning that any scheme of irrigation in the district of Christiana was liable to be delayed. Without the certainty of a regular supply of water any scheme of settlement would be a hazardous enterprise, and Milner's advice that the colonists should postpone their departure was a wise one in the circumstances. (53)

It was accepted with resignation in Chubut, but not with undue pessimism. A request from Harford, the British Minister in Buenos Aires, for a list of prospective emigrants indicated that the British Government was desirous of furthering the scheme. There was a feeling that the problem of water was not insoluble, and that what was more pertinent to the success of the emigration plan was the finalization of the conditions governing the establishment of the Welsh settlement at Christiana.

Harford had already discussed the situation with the Chubut delegates after their arrival in Buenos Aires from South Africa.

"From what Mr. D. S. Jones and Mr. R. J. Roberts, the Welsh delegates to South Africa, said to me when here in July, they were dissatisfied with the offer made to them by the Transvaal authorities. They especially wished for more land capable of irrigation than it was prepared to allot them. They also said that the proposed mode of irrigation had not seemed to them a good one, and that they had been assured that the question would be gone into again. Though having no scientific training both these gentlemen have great practical knowledge of irrigation from their long residence in Chubut." (54) "The Welsh delegates," he wrote in another letter, "are very good at driving a bargain I should say, from what I saw of them and know of Welshmen generally. If they don't get what they want, more good land, i.e. land capable of irrigation, I really believe they will stay where they are - or go to Canada. They seemed dissatisfied with the offer made them, and are waiting for a reply to their counter offer. With this the [Transvaal] Land Commission are acquainted, they say, in the letters I enclose in my despatch. They thought the Transvaal poor arid, no better if not worse than at Chubut, where animals live somehow on wretched pasturage as it never rains at Chubut practically. Only horses, asses and mules can be exported from this country [Argentine] at present owing to foot and mouth disease. This is a further complication and reason for delay."(55)

Four months went by and still there was no reply from the Transvaal Government to the counter-proposals of the Chubut delegates. The delay seemed inexplicable to the South African Emigration Committee, and it stirred its members into seeking intervention from other quarters, even the Argentine Government itself, which invited Harford to clarify the situation. "The Argentine Minister of Commerce, who appears to have been consulted in the matter, has asked Mr. Harford whether the British authorities will assent to these counter proposals and, if so, whether the emigrants will obtain free passages and be allowed to take part of their stock and implements. On the receipt of a reply, the number of families and quantity of stock for which passages will have to be provided, will be reported." (56)

For its part the Colonial Office in London had been active during these months in making inquiries as to the most effective way of transporting the settlers to South Africa. Acting upon Lord Milner's latest estimate that some sixty families, three hundred people in all, would opt to emigrate to Christiana, (57) it had instructed the Crown agents to approach certain shipping firms and invite tenders for the conveyance of settlers and stock. It resulted from all the correspondence and discussions entailed by these inquiries that there were two possibilities; either the settlers could be brought to England and thence carried to Capetown, or they could be transported directly to that place from Buenos Aires. There was a meticulous scrutiny of the expenses involved before the Colonial Office came to a decision. "It would be much longer and more expensive, though apparently not quite so much more expensive as one would have supposed, to bring the people round via Liverpool. But the chief objection to this course is the great difficulty of transferring the settlers from Liverpool to Southampton; indeed . . . if these people wish to take with them heavy impedimenta such as farm implements and carts and possibly live stock, the difficulty seems almost insuperable . . . The cost of the transfer will probably amount to something like £4,000, possibly more if the settlers take heavy stock with them, and we shall have to tell Lord Milner that payment must be made out of the loan."(58) The provisional date for the transportation of the colonists was June, 1903, but Chamberlain was still insistent that no definitive arrangements could be entered into until Milner had signified his acquiescence, and was able to confirm that the outstanding difficulty regarding the disposal of the Vaal river water had been finally cleared up.

VII

To wait upon events, as the Colonial Office seemed disposed to do, ran counter to the sentiments that had infused the Chubut settlers with enthusiasm for repatriation to British territory. But even they had realized that it would be unwise to act upon the assumption that it was in order for them to proceed with their plans, pending an official confirmation from London and Pretoria that all obstacles had been removed. After considering a request from the British Legation in Buenos Aires for a complete list of intending emigrants, the South African Emigration Committee decided to issue a further statement to clarify the position as it appeared to them and to forward it to the Legation.

In a covering letter it was stated that "the Committee are of opinion that it will be most advisable to know definitely the terms of settlement in the Transvaal so that we may submit a full text to intending emigrants, but as the matter stands now, we think it will be detrimental to the movement to ask for the names of the adults, etc, of settlers as we have nothing definite to put before them, and as soon as we receive a reply we will forward you a full report by first opportunity." (59)

The statement, which accompanied this letter, disclaimed any rumours which were apparently circulating in the Argentine that the settlers were ready to leave for South Africa, and regretted that the British authorities should have been misinformed in that respect. It requested some assurance on three points: that the British Government would accede to the proposals submitted by the Chubut delegates to the Land Commission in the Transvaal; provide free passage for the emigrants; and allow them to take part of their implements and live stock. "Needless for us to say that the colonists are in such pecuniary circumstances at present owing to the successive floods of the last four years, and ruinous effects has made it impossible for them to go to South Africa on their own resources. Also . . . that on its becoming known of people intending to leave the place, everyone takes an undue advantage of them when trying to dispose of their effects, of which they will not receive one fourth the value, as was the case with those who left for Canada, and this will greatly cripple them to start with any degree of success in South Africa where stock and implements are at such high prices." (60)

VIII

Under the impression, perhaps, that the statement was not clear enough, a second letter was sent to the British Legation enclosing copies of the proposals and counter-proposals as they had emerged from the negotiations in Pretoria. "By your inquiry for the particulars concerning number of people and stock, some of our people here are too ready to believe that the (British) Government is going to transport them and their stock free to South Africa. As you know by our papers (of which I enclose copies) that we did not come to a definite agreement with the Transvaal authorities, we must come to better understanding on some particular points before we can proceed safely." These points concerned the possibility of a bigger grant of irrigable land than 50 acres, a more definite price as to the land itself, terms of transportation to South Africa, and an agreement that the payment of the first instalment on the land should be demanded after the expiry of twelve months from the date on which the settler was supplied with adequate water to irrigate his holding. "I believe that a clear understanding on these points would avoid a great deal of trouble." (61)

Together with these communications, which were distinctly cautious and non-commital in tone, there were others which discussed with less circumspection the various possibilities of chartering steamers to convey the settlers to South Africa. But all that Harford felt himself called upon to do, in reply to this correspondence, was to warn the South African Emigration Committee periodically that the problem of water supply still defied solution. It was probably with some relief that he heard that the emigrants would not be in a position to leave Chubut until June, 1904. (62)

On October 31, Llwyd ap Iwan returned from South Africa. For four months he had remained in the Transvaal awaiting a report from a Government expert on the prospects of irrigation at Christiana. The information passed on to him must have convinced him that he was simply kicking his heels in Pretoria, for he decided to leave that town on October 2. He spent five days in Capetown and then booked his return passage in the *Langton Grange,* the same ship which had brought him and his fellow delegates, with their vision of a Welsh colony in South Africa, from Buenos Aires some eleven months earlier. He called on the British Legation in the Argentine capital, and expounded to Harford the problems that were jeopardizing the whole emigration scheme. "The last delegate told me that it was a question if the Transvaal authorities could use the water of the river (the Vaal, I think) for irrigation, as the neighbouring state of Natal, I suppose, had water rights and objected. This has to be decided before anything can be done, and the expense of irrigation will be very large." (63) Llwyd also put in a claim for travelling expenses which was duly paid by the Colonial Office, and was back in Chubut by the middle of November. His report to the South African Emigration Committee could only reinforce the feeling in the colony that the dispute between the Governments of the Transvaal and Cape Colony was degenerating into a stalemate that might well dissipate any hope of finding a new home in South Africa.

IX

The new year began on a gloomy note. In a letter to Alfred
Lyttleton who had replaced Joseph Chamberlain as Colonial
Secretary, Lord Milner had little to say about the emigration
scheme that was encouraging, and his observations afforded
one explanation why the counter-proposals of the Chubut delegates had not favourably impressed the Government of the
Transvaal. "The Irrigation schemes under contemplation have
not been sufficiently developed to render the consideration of
the question of such settlers expedient, and I may point out
that some considerable time must elapse before the schemes
can be carried out and the land made available for settlement.
With regard to what are termed the counter proposals to this
Administration, I would point out that the letter from the
Commissioner of Lands contained the proposals of this
Administration and was sent after due consideration of the
delegates' letter of the 6th April and a long personal interview
with them at which the subject was fully discussed. The general
terms laid down in the letter of the 24 April last must be adhered to, as it is impossible to submit more specific terms until
the Irrigation schemes are more advanced and the Administration is in a position to gauge the cost of such works. Taking all
things into consideration, I am inclined to think that the matter
should rest in abeyance for the present, and when the
Administration is in a position to receive the Chubut immigrants, the terms and conditions to be offered them can then
form the subject of negotiations." (64) Milner requested that
the South African Emigration Committee should be informed
of his views. This was done, but whatever form that
communication took, it did not include the laconic comment of
the Colonial Office on Milner's letter that "this is probably the
end of the scheme."

Not a few people in Chubut itself were thinking along the same lines and adjusting themselves to the idea that they could expend their energy more profitably at home than indulge in visionary schemes of colonizing an unknown tract of land in South Africa. This reorientation of attitude did not pass unnoticed at the British Legation in Buenos Aires. "From what I hear from people in the South," Harford wrote to a friend, "I expect very few, if any, Welsh will emigrate to South Africa. They are doing very well now in Chubut, good crops, no floods, and the Argentine Government are helping. They make a lot of money by exporting hay made of *alfalfa* (lucerne) which has already been tried with great success. It is used in the south of the Republic where it can be grown. South Africa did not impress the Welsh delegates. Land is poor there and every kind of disease and insect do prey on crops . . . I cannot believe the Welsh are doing anything but "bluffing" so as to get the Argentine Government to induce them to stay by offering every kind of help. I know the Welsh well; they can drive a bargain against anyone."(65) It was not the first time that Harford had detected, or thought he had discovered, a predilection for bargaining amongst the Chubut Welsh. It may have amused him, a feeling not shared by his superiors in London who were becoming slightly irritated by the whole business of Welsh emigration. "It appears from this letter," ran one comment on it," that the Welsh settlers at Chubut, about whom we have had a good deal of trouble, prefer Argentine to South Africa."

The months of silence that followed seemed to confirm the conclusion drawn by the Colonial Office that the colonists had had second thoughts about engaging themselves in a venture which promised less security than what they already enjoyed in Patagonia. But there were still a few settlers uncompromisingly committed to the emigration scheme and who expected a reciprocal solidarity of purpose from London. If Lyttleton needed any evidence of their pertinacity, he found it in a letter addressed to him in the late autumn of 1904. "My brother and myself with others, practical farmers in irrigation, feel very anxious to know how the Canal and other matters connected with the land in Christiana in the Transvaal,

South Africa, are progressing, and if there is any likelihood for us to be allowed to immigrate there at an early date. It may not be out of place for me to mention that we constructed canals of scores of miles. My brother is at present in Wales on a visit to our relations, and I send this through his medium because we are not certain if any correspondence from Welshmen in this colony would ever reach its destination to any M.P. in Great Britain for reasons better withheld. An early answer would greatly oblige and relieve our anxious minds." (66) To this earnest enquiry the Colonial Office could only reply that there had been no fresh developments in South Africa since the beginning of the year.

It is perhaps strange that, in these unpromising circumstances, the South African Emigration Committee did not pay more attention to the possibilities of another scheme laid before them by Owen Thomas,* a Welshman who was to earn much distinction as agricultural specialist, soldier and politician before his death. Like Captain Vaughan, Thomas was in South Africa when hostilities broke out. He was given the rank of colonel, and within a short time raised an irregular body of cavalry, the Prince of Wales's Light Horse, which distinguished itself for its fighting qualities and successes in the field. It was singularly unfortunate that towards the end of his military career an attempt should have been made to implicate him in an alleged scandal concerning the recruitment of men in Australia and New Zealand for the Light Horse. Thomas insisted that the matter should be thoroughly investigated by the War Office, and was completely exonerated from all charges. (67)

Thomas's real interest, however, lay in farming and its problems, which he had had the opportunity of studying at first hand in Britain during the four years spent by him as member of the Royal Commission on agricultural depression in 1893-97. Upon relinquishing the command of the Light Horse, he decided to concentrate his attention on evolving plans for land settlement in the newly acquired Boer territories. He entered

* later General Sir Owen Thomas.

into correspondence with Lord Milner on the subject, and eventually accepted an invitation to go to Johannesburg to examine the scheme of settlement proposed by the Land Board which Milner had recently set up in the Transvaal and the Orange River Colony.

In the light of his intimate knowledge of the Boer lands during two and a half years of intensive campaigning, the scheme appeared to him totally unrealistic and the ignorance and incompetence of the Land Board appalling. Neither did Milner escape his strictures. "He seems to me to be under the impression that once the conditions of tenure are arranged to the satisfaction of all concerned the scheme will work automatically, and that the only thing required by the Board will be to buy land, select the tenants or settlers and receive rents, etc. These I consider a very simple matter compared to the general management of the property, the guidance and superintendence required to keep good men on the land. This country has so many drawbacks such as rinderpest, locusts, red water, heart water, drought, hailstones, etc; any of these things might ruin a really good settler the first year, and as the Government's object is a political one, the settlers should be well cared for by experienced and sympathetic men."(68)

It was early in 1903 that Owen Thomas met the three Chubut delegates who had newly arrived in the Transvaal. A thorough Welshman, he was able to understand their aspirations of founding a Welsh colony, but could also appreciate that they and their fellow colonists were the type of experienced and hard-headed settlers who deserved every encouragement to come to South Africa. It was after discussing their problems that he visited Rhodesia, and was convinced by what he saw and heard there that it was the only country capable of affording the best political and economic conditions and the most advanced facilities for a permanent and viable settlement.

In 1904 Thomas returned to England to publish a report on South Africa entitled *Agricultural and Pastoral Prospects of South Africa,* in which he incorporated his favourable impressions of Rhodesia, but which was to lead to an unexpected and disturbing incident in his public career. (69) It was in London too that he heard of the inconclusive negotiations between the Transvaal Government and the Chubut delegates, and the return of the latter to the Argentine. To him it seemed an opportune moment to paint an attractive picture of what the Chubut Welsh might hope to enjoy in Rhodesia, if they chose to be guided by him.

This he did in a letter to one of the delegates, R. J. Roberts. Summarizing the results of his survey of Rhodesia, he assured Roberts that Rhodesia was superior in every way to the Transvaal. With only a population of 10,000 whites in an area covering 750,000 square miles, and with few of those engaged in farming, there was such an abundance of good agricultural land that the authorities were prepared to bestow 2000 acres gratuitously on a settler. Although primarily suitable for stock-breeding, the land could be exploited by an enterprising farmer for the cultivation of cotton, tobacco, sugar in addition to cereals, and 2000 miles of railroads had already been constructed to link the countryside with the main centres of population and industry. Thomas proposed that the South African Emigration Committee should send delegates to Rhodesia to examine the prospects of a settlement, as they had done in the case of the Transvaal. He opined that there would be no difficulty in obtaining a grant of 200 square miles for the establishment of such a settlement. If this were achieved, and a group of Chubut Welsh definitely settled in Rhodesia, he would undertake to persuade a number of their countrymen from Wales itself to join them in their venture and found a Welsh colony "in every sense of the word." (70)

No evidence has been forthcoming that Thomas's letter had any discernible effect on the Committee. It certainly did not deflect its members from their original intention of going to the Transvaal, or it may have arrived too late for them to revise their plans. What they did reconsider, and finally discard, were the counter-proposals to which they had tenaciously adhered since the return of their delegates from South Africa, and which they now felt were as much a threat to the emigration scheme as the dispute over the waters of the River Vaal. In a letter to G. R. Hughes, Secretary of the Land Commission in the Transvaal, the Secretary of the Emigration Committee, J. G. Jones, accepted unreservedly the conditions laid down by the Government of the Transvaal: "We hereby inform you that we accept the terms stated in your letter of the 24th April, 1903, viz, 50 acres of irrigable land and 500 acres of dry land.*

We beg to ask you, would it not be advisable to transport the intending emigrants from here to Christiana previous to the completion of the Vaal weir and canal, as it would take some time for us to build the necessary homesteads, etc, and to prepare the land to receive the water from the canal. Otherwise we are of opinion that the indefinite delay will materially inconvenience and paralyze the [emigration] movement, and should you consider the above project expedient, we would suggest June 1906 as the most appropriate date to leave here, thereby allowing nearly two years for the necessary survey and commencement of the work.

Inasmuch as the Committee are continually asked what is the price of the land and what will be the cost of the weir and canal, we beg to ask is it not possible for you to forward us the estimate cost of such works, also the price of the land and what amount of acreage will the proposed scheme irrigate, as it will considerably assist us to make up the necessary list of intending settlers, which has been asked by his Excellency the British Minister in Buenos Aires. Also the above information will silence those who are trying by all devices to stop the movement." (71)

Some idea as to the nature of these devices was revealed in another letter addressed by J. G. Jones to the British Minister in the Argentine capital on the subject of the Christiana settlement. "Doubtless it seems strange that we are again asking for the estimate of cost works, etc., but as we have said before there is a certain class here whom [sic] are trying their utmost to destroy the movement by saying the settlers will be saddled with an unbearable burden for life. We therefore beseech your good

* See *supra* pp. 134-5, and footnote.

offices on our behalf and to make it known in the proper
quarters. Needless for us to inform you that we have experienced another disastrous flood this year which has ruined
the major part of our canals, etc., thereby depriving us of our
harvest for the ensuing season." (72)

Within less than a year the hopes of the South African
Emigration Committee and its adherents had crumbled away.
Early in 1905, Lord Milner resigned his office as Governor of
the Transvaal and returned to England, but not before he had
reiterated his discouraging views on the Christiana project.
"The Engineer in charge of the survey is being exclusively
employed in drawing up the Christiana Irrigation Scheme, and
after the scheme is submitted, it will probably be necessary to
ascertain if the adjoining colonies will share in it. The preliminaries will naturally take time to settle, and when they are
decided it is estimated that at least two years will elapse before
the canal can be put into operation. In these circumstances, I
am inclined to think that the reopening of negotiations with the
Chubut settlers should rest with the Transvaal Administration, and this course was recently suggested to the Secretary of
the Chubut Emigration Committee in reply to an enquiry on
the subject addressed direct to the Commissioner of Lands."
(73)

Certainly, in the circumstances, it was the only wise and
practical course of action, for events were to prove that even at
the end of 1905, despite large-scale investigations by surveyors
and engineers, the decision whether to proceed with the
Christiana irrigation plan was left in abeyance. (74) In Chubut
it may be surmised that the vision of a Welsh colony in South
Africa gradually waned until it became an unattainable ideal
amongst a few irreconcilable spirits. "From recent reports
received from Chubut," ran a dispatch from the British
Legation in Buenos Aires, "it would seem that, with the exception of some malcontents, there is no general desire on the part
of the Welsh settlers to emigrate. The Chubut Mercantile
Company in May last caused a statement to be published by
their agents, Messrs. John Edwards & Co. of Liverpool, in the

Times and other English papers, denying that there was any intention on the part of the settlers to break up the colony and to emigrate to Rhodesia and elsewhere." (75)

The cryptic comment of the Foreign Office on this particular passage in the dispatch scarcely concealed the feeling of relief in official quarters: "Welsh settlers in Chubut contented now."

Notes

Part 1

Struggle and Disillusionment

(1) F. O. 6/420, pp. 39-40. Inclosure 9 in No. 27.

(2) *Ibid,* pp. 11-12. Inclosure 1 in No. 9.

(3) F.O.6/502, pp. 579-84. Thornton to Earl Russell, dated July 25, 1865.

(4) F.O.6/260. Letter from the Government Emigration Officer in Liverpool, dated May 27, 1865.

That the Patagonian venture was ill-informed and ill-planned and jeopardized from the outset by ignorance of the physical and climatic features of the Chubut region has been exposed by Professor E. G. Bowen. *See* his *The Welsh Colony in Patagonia,* 1865-1885 in the *Geographical Journal,* Vol. 132, Part 1, March 1966, pp. 16-27.

Professor Alun Davies has re-examined the attitude of Michael D. Jones towards Welsh emigration to Patagonia and his motives in supporting it. *See* his *Michael D. Jones a'r Wladfa* in the *Transactions of the Honourable Society of Cymmrodorion.* 1966, Part 1, pp. 73-87.

(5) A good proportion of the settlers were miners and artisans. Six years later, in 1871, when the population numbered 153, there were 11 colliers, 4 carpenters, 2 masons,1 brickmaker, 1 bookseller, but only 1 farmer and 3 farm labourers. (F.O.6/302, p. 299).

(6) F.O.6/262. Ford to the Earl of Clarendon, dated April 22, 1866.

(7) F.O.6/261. Foreign Office to Ford, dated June 5, 1866.

(8) F.O.6/263, pp. 89-96 and 108-121. Watson's Reports of July 10 and July 14, 1866.

(9) F.O.6/302, pp. 252-279. Report on the Chubut Colony, April 17, 1871.

(10) F.O.6/267, pp. 189-190. Matthew to Lord Stanley, dated June 12, 1867.

(11) F.O.6/284, p. 131. The war lasted over four years and cost the Argentine £8,700,000.

(12) F.O.6/291, p. 308.

(13) F.O.6/302, p. 31. MacDonnell to Earl Granville, dated February 8, 1871. Between 1865 and 1870 at least 58 British subjects resident in the Argentine had been murdered. (F.O.6/293, pp. 190-92).

(14) F.O.6/303, pp. 227-232.

(15) There was an exchange of polemics on this subject in the *Letters concerning the country of the Argentine Republic,* published in London in 1869, which referred to the Chubut colony and its fluctuating fortunes. One of the letters makes the interesting suggestion that the Argentine Government had supported the establishment of the colony in the hope that eventually the settlers would secure the region as the result, presumably, of the periodic arrival of new immigrants.

(16) "Many of them (the Indians) had been accustomed to visit the Welsh colony at the Chupat for trade, and, in their opinion, as afterwards expressed to me, the honest Welsh colonists were much pleasanter and safer to deal with than the

'Christians' of the Rio Negro. They seemed to have been especially impressed with the size and excellence of the home-made loaves, one of which would be given in return for half a guanaco: and Jackechan (the Chief) often expatiated on the liberality of the colonists and the goodness of their breed. These men also felt strongly the kindness with which an Indian, if overtaken with rum, would be covered up or carried into an outhouse by the Chupat people; whereas at the Rio Negro the only attention paid to him would be to strip and plunder him completely." Musters, *At Home with the Patagonians,* p. 113. The author goes on to say that this Chief carried on his person a photograph of Lewis Jones with whom he was on the friendliest terms.

(17)   F.O.6/302, pp. 119-124. MacDonnell to Earl Granville, dated March 16, 1871.

(18)   F.O.6/303, pp. 149-161. MacDonnell to Earl Granville, dated October 28, 1871.

(19)   *Ibid,* p. 169. A copy and translation of the petition and of the Argentine Government's reply were transmitted to the Foreign Office by MacDonnell in his despatch of October 28, 1971.

(20)   This replaced the Law of September 29, 1857, which granted the children of foreigners the privilege of choosing their nationality at a certain age.

(21)   F.O.6/309, pp. 104-5. Michael D. Jones to the British Minister in Buenos Aires, dated October 25, 1871.

(22)   Captain Dennistoun was in command of H.M.S. *Cracker* which visited the colony in April, 1871. His report contained a comprehensive account of the state of the community, and although insistent upon certain deficiencies, was not entirely discouraging.

(23)   F.O.5/1373. Archibald to Earl Granville, dated March 30, 1872.

(24)   F.O.6/312. "Gwasanaethu y Wladfa yn ymob modd o fewn ei allu nes daw y Wladfa Gymreig yn Deyrnas Gymreig gadarn". The head office of the Company was at Rhuthin in North Wales, and was managed by the Rev. D. Lloyd Jones. *(Y Drych,* April 11, 1872).

(25)   *Ibid.* "Mae arch Seisnig fawr wedi cael gwneyd i ni fel cenedl, ond y mae yr hen Gymry yn gwrthod gorwedd yn dawel tra byddo'r Saeson yn sicrhau y clawr." *(ditto)*

(26)   F.O.6/324, pp. 205-10. Their numbers had declined from 79, 712 in 1873 to 68, 277 in 1874.

(27)   F.O.6/326, p. 197.

(28)   F.O.6/318. MacDonnell to the Foreign Office, dated January 29, 1873.

(29)   F.O.6/333. Report of Captain Fairfax of H.M.S. *Volage* after his visit to Chubut in February, 1876.

(3)   Beerbohn, *Wanderings in Patagonia,* pp. 267-276.

(31)   F.O.6/333. Ford to the Marquess of Salisbury, dated April 18, 1879.

(32)   F.O.6/359, p. 249. October 14, 1880.

(33)   F.O.6/361, p. 26. Rumbold to Earl Granville, dated July 13, 1880.

(34)   *Ibid,* pp. 31-32. Rumbold to Earl Granville, dated October 9, 1880.

(35)   *Ibid,* pp. 277-80. Captain Erskine's Report on the Chubut colony, April 21, 1880.

(36)   F.O.6/377, pp. 128-133. The Bishop of Falkland to Earl Granville, dated June 28, 1883.

(37)   F.O.6/379, pp. 121-124. Monson to Earl Granville, dated July 1, 1884. According to the confidential report of Commander Fullerton of H.M.S. *Algerine* some of the Indian tribes friendly to the Welsh were decoyed to Chubut

under false pretences, forced on board a steamer and conveyed to Buenos Aires where the women and children were distributed as domestic servants and the men sent to work on the coast. The callous treatment to which they were subjected while being driven through Chubut roused vigorous protests amongst the Welsh, which further exacerbated the none too amicable relations between the settlers and Argentine officialdom. (F.O.6/383, p. 186).

(38)   *Ibid,* pp. 95-97. Monson to Earl Granville, dated June 16, 1884.

(39)   *Ibid,* pp. 111-113. Monson to Earl Granville, dated July 1, 1884.

(40)   *Ibid,* pp. 177-8. Monson to Earl Granville, dated August 1, 1884.

(41)   *Ibid,* p. 243. Monson to Earl Granville, dated August 30, 1884.

(42)   F.O.6/383, pp. 81-82. Lewis Jones to Love Jones Parry, dated January 15, 1884.

(43)   F.O.6/397, pp. 58-60. Report by Captain Kennedy, senior officer on South-East coast of America, dated May 27, 1887.

(44)   F.O.6/418, p. 391. It was estimated that the Argentine's domestic and foreign debts in 1891 amounted to £74,000,000, and its revenue to only £6,000,000. After meeting the interest on certain debts, the Government was left with only £1,500,000 to defray its expenses.

(45)   N.L.W. MSS 18427C. R. J. Berwyn to Tobit Evans, dated August 25, 1866. "Os na ddaw Cymry allan bydd cenhedloedd eraill yn dod. Maent yn dod o un i un, Hyn yw ein pryder. Gwyddom am eangderoedd gwychion yn nghanol y wlad ganwaith mwy na'r dyffryn lle yr ydym. Ond nid doeth udganu hyn neu daw Italiaid neu Rwsiaid o'r tu ol i ni."

(46)   F.O.6/407, p. 167.

(47)   F.O.6/427, pp. 277-8.

(48)   F.O.6/444, pp. 17-25. Report on Chubut by Commander R. R. Neeld of H.M.S. *Beagle,* January 29, 1895.

(49)   F.O.6/496, pp. 1-14. Statement on Patagonia signed in London, February 14, 1899, by Llwyd ap Iwan and T. Benbow Phillips.

(50)   Pinto-Duschinsky, *The Political Thought of Lord Salisbury,* p. 134.

(51)   F.O.6/459, pp. 34-5. Barrington to the Foreign Office, dated February 28, 1899.

(52)   F.O.6/496, p. 20. Memorandum of March 9, 1899.

(53)   *Ibid,* p. 42.

(54)   F.O.6/461, pp. 46-9 and 85-7. Vice-Admiral Brent to the Foreign Office, dated March 11 and September 13, 1899.

(55)   M.P.s for Swansea, East Glamorgan and Denbigh respectively.

(56)   F.O.6/496, p. 18. Minute by St. John Broderick to Lord Salisbury, dated April 25, 1899.

(57)   *Ibid,* pp. 25-40. Brynmor Jones to St. John Broderick, dated April 25, 2899.

(58)   *Ibid,* pp. 22-3. Observations by W. E. Davidson on the Welsh statement and petition, dated April 26, 1899. A previous communication (*Ibid,* pp. 15-16) tersely pointed out that Lewis Jones had flatly turned down the proposal for nominating him as Vice-Consul in 1880. The implication here is that he had thereby let fall an opportunity to prove that the British Government had more than a nominal interest in the colony.

(59)   F.O.6/459, p. 8. Foreign Office to Barrington, dated May 8, 1899.

(60)   *Ibid,* pp. 86-8. Barrington to the Foreign Office, dated June 22, 1889.

(61)   *Parliamentary Debates,* Vol. LXXV, p. 230. July 25, 1899.

(62)   F.O.6/462, pp. 70-8. Report on Chubut by Captain Charles Cochran of H.M.S. *Pegasus,* July 1, 1899.

(63) Amongst other eminent colonists ruined by the floods was the father of Eluned (Morgan), later a well known Welsh Patagonian author, who found herself forced to seek employment in Wales. (N.L.W. MSS 18427C, letter dated February, 1900).

(64) F.O.6/496, pp. 76-88. Report on Chubut by the commander of H.M.S. *Basilick,* dated May, 1901.

(65) *Ibid,* pp. 54-59. Confidential report by F. S. Clarke to the Marquess of Lansdowne, dated February 22, 1901.

(66) *Ibid,* pp. 76-88, *op cit.* Also F.O.6/474, pp. 221-3 and F.O.6/477, pp. 38-49. On the basis of these complaints the Chargé d' Affaires in Buenos Aires was instructed to submit a memorandum to the Argentine Government drawing its attention to them. (F.O.6/496, pp. 229-30 and 263-66).

(67) F.O.6/477, pp. 34-6. Hugh Davies, Welsh chaplain in Chubut, to the Marquess of Lansdowne, dated May 13, 1902.

(68) F.O.6/468, pp. 51-52. John Morley to F. S. Clarke, dated January 9, 1901.

(69) *Ibid,* pp. 55-6. Governor Conesa to the Argentine Minister of the Interior, dated January 11, 1901.

(70) *Ibid,* pp. 58-60. *Standard* of January 15, 1901.

(71) The news of Morley's misfortune reached London in due course and prompted D. A. Thomas, M.P. for Merthyr Tydfil, to ask in the House of Commons whether the British Government was aware of the allegations made against the Chubut police. Viscount Cranbourne, the Secretary of Foreign Affairs, was content to reply that representations had been made to the Argentine Government by the British Chargé d' Affaires in Buenos Aires, and that Morley, the person most affected by the incident, thought them to be valuable and efficacious. *Parliamentary Debates,* Vol. LXXXIX, 1901, p. 305.

(72) F.O.6/468 *op cit,* pp. 58-60.

(73) F.O.6/462, pp. 81-8. Report of Commander R. Groome of H.M.S. *Flora,* July 4, 1900.

(74) Richard's report was regarded with some scepticism by the British Government, which came to the conclusion that it would be inadvisable to publish it on account of what it considered to be certain tendentious passages relating to the grievances of the Welsh settlers. Richards does not seem to have been entirely disconcerted by the open hint that he had been somewhat selective in his presentation of facts, and explained that he was anxious for the sake of the Conservative Government as well as for the improvement of the settlers' lot that something should be done to facilitate the projected emigration from Chubut. "By so doing I am convinced that it (the Government) would strengthen its position in Wales. It would disarm some and put to shame others of its Welsh Parliamentary opponents. If one or two of these gentlemen knew the contents of my Report, they would not be anxious for its publication . . . With regard to the Welsh Press, I should like to persue *(sic)* some policy that would strengthen the hands of the present Government, while at the same time I should be serving the higher interests of my deluded and unfortunate fellow-countrymen in Chubut." (F.O.6/470, pp. 106-7. Rev. R. Richards to Eric Barrington, (brother of Sir William Barrington) at the Foreign Office, dated May 31, 1901. *See also* F.O.6/496, pp. 96 and 121-3; and *Parliamentary Debates,* Vol. XCVI, p. 787, July 4, 1901.

(75) F.O.6/496, pp. 76-88. Report of Commander Dodgson of H.M.S. *Basilick,* May, 1901.

(76) F.O.6/477, pp. 34-6. Hugh Davies to the Marquess of Lansdowne, dated May 13, 1902.
(77) The best study of the beginnings and consequent development of the Welsh colony in Chubut is *Y Wladfa* by R. Bryn Williams, who has consulted Welsh and Spanish documentary and printed sources.

Part 2

Call from Canada

(1) C.O.45/828, pp. 125-8. Report by W. L. Griffith, dated January 5, 1899.

(2) Lewis H. Thomas. "Lloyd George's visit to the North West, 1899." Saskatchewan History, Vol. III, Winter 1950, No. 1, pp. 17-22. The report is also published in C.O.45/865, Part II, pp. 11-18.

(3) C.O.45/845, Part II, pp. 25-6. Report by W. L. Griffith, dated December 4, 1899.

(4) Ibid, pp. 19-26. Report by W. T. R. Preston, dated September 14, 1900.

(5) C.O.45/865, Part II, pp. 19-26.

(6) C.O.45/828, pp. 125-8.

(7) C.O.42/884, p. 822. Minute dated August 9, 1901.

(8) Ibid, pp. 823-4 and C.O.42/885, p. 511, August 9-16, 1901. See also F.O.6/468, pp. 18-19, 22 and 176.

(9) C.O.42/885, pp. 656-7. Barrington to the Foreign Office, dated September 26, 1901.

(10) C.O.42/890, pp. 57-60. Report by Ernest Scott, dated September 15, 1901.

(11) Ibid

(12) C.O.42/891. L.22. The expenses of the Patagonian mission came to 2,336 dollars.

(13) F.O.6/496, p. 155.

(14) Western Mail, February 11 and 14, 1902. This and the newspaper extracts that follow have been taken from N.L.W. MSS 10816.

(15) Yorkshire Post, February 18, 1902.

(16) Standard, February 10, 1902.

(17) Daily Telegraph, February 19, 1902.

(18) Western Mail, February 14, 1902. See also F.O.6/496, p. 155.

(19) It included Sir Alfred Thomas, Chairman of the Welsh Parliamentary Party, Sir John Llewelyn, the Bishops of Bangor and St. David's, Dr. Isambard Owen, Senior Deputy-Chancellor of the University of Wales, the Hon. George Kenyon, Brynmor Jones, M.P., S. T. Davies, M.P., Reginald McKenna, M.P., William Abraham (Mabon) M.P., Keir Hardie, M.P., The Mayors of Cardiff, Swansea and Aberystwyth, Richard Cory, the Director of Cory Brothers, Cardiff, William Davies, Editor of the Western Mail, David Davies, Editor of the South Wales Daily Post, Vincent Evans, Secretary of the Honourable Society of the Cymmrodorion, Rev. G. Hartwell Jones, Rev. J. Ll. Thomas, the Vicar of Aberpergwm, Llewelyn Williams, and many others of note. It is interesting to record that other Welsh public figures who expressed their support for the emigration scheme but were unable to be present were Sir James Hills-Johnes, Sir John Williams, M.D., Sir Lewis Morris, Professor John Rhys, Principal of Jesus College, Oxford, Sir Charles Philips, of Picton Castle, Pembrokeshire, The Right Hon. Lord Llangattock, and Sir Henry M. Stanley.

(20) The fullest account of the meeting at the Colonial Office was published in the *Western Mail,* February 19, 1902 and the *South Wales Daily News* of the same date.

(21) *Belfast Evening Telegraph,* February 19, 1902.

(22) *St. James Gazette,* February 20, 1902.

(23) *Freeman's Journal,* February 20, 1902.

(24) *Western Mail,* February 21, 1902.

(25) *Daily Telegraph,* March 7, 1902.

(26) C.O.42/889, pp. 314-321. Report of Commander Edmund Jervoise of H.M.S. *Nymphe,* dated May 23, 1902.

(27) *Western Mail,* February 28, 1902.

(28) *Cardiff Times,* March 1, 1902.

(29) *Llangollen Advertiser,* February 28, 1902.

(30) *South Wales Daily News,* April 11, 1902. The author of the letter was Caswodyn Rhys, who had returned to Swansea after spending 15 years in Patagonia.

(31) Gell MSS. *Letters and Papers.* Thomas Rhys to Lyttelton Gell, dated February 13, 1902.

(32) *Ibid.* Rhys to Gell, dated February 17, 1902.

(33) *Ibid.* Rhys to Gell, dated February 23, 1902.

(34) *Ibid.* Rhys to Gell, dated March 3, 1902.

(35) *Western Mail,* April 11, 1902.

(36) C.O.45/901. Report by W. L. Griffith, dated July 17, 1902.

(37) C.O.42/889. Extract included in the Report of Commander Edmund Jervoise, dated May 23, 1902, *op cit.*

(38) *Carnarvon Herald,* May 23, 1902, published a summary and extracts from the letters contributed by Rev. D. Lloyd Jones to the *Drafod.*

(39) The actual number of emigrants varied according to reports. *The Western Mail,* June 11, 1902 speaks of nearly 300, other papers of 256, and Commander Jervoise's Report places them at 239. The tables published by the Quebec Agent show that 233 Welsh immigrants arrived at that port, (C.O.45/901, Part II p. 67), but there is reason to believe that some of the original party were left behind at Liverpool on account of illness and, possibly, other motives.

(40) C.O.42/889, pp. 314-321. Report of Commander Jervoise *op cit.*

(41) *Western Mail,* June 11, 1902.

(42) Amongst those who attended the reception were the eminent Welsh preachers, J. O. Williams (Pedrog), David Adams and Peter Price, the poet and Eisteddfod conductor, Llew Tegid, and the founder and editor of rhe *Cymro,* Isaac Foulkes (Llyfrbryf).

(43) *Western Mail,* June 13, 1902.

(44) *Ibid.*

(45) *Ibid.*

(46) *Manchester Guardian,* June 21, 1902. Letter from W. L. Griffith.

(47) Gilbert Johnson. "The Patagonian Welsh." *Saskatchewan History* Vol. XVI, Autumn 1963, No. 3. *See also* Edward McCourt *Saskatchewan,* p. 114, where Jenkins is described as a "bubbly energetic little Welshman."

(48) *An Official Handbook of Information relating to the Dominion of Canada,* January 1890, pp. 71-72. *See also Tracts relating to Canada* 1888-1893. *Dominion of Canada. Manitoba and the North West Territories* Report by P. R. Ritchie, 1892.

146   CRISIS IN CHUBUT

(49) *Saskatchewan History,* Vol. 1. May 1948, No. 2. p. 24.
(50) McCourt *Saskatchewan op cit,* p. 114.
(51) Lewis H. Thomas. "From the Pampas to the Prairies." *Saskatchewan history* Vol. XXIV. Winter 1971, No. 1. pp. 10-12.
(52) C.O.417/53, pp. 848-849. A. O. Vaughan to the Colonial Office, dated September 8, 1902.
(53) *Western Mail.* June 16, 1902.
(54) *Ibid.*
(55) Lewis H. Thomas, *op cit.*

Part 3

South African vision

(1) Lockhard and Woodhouse. *Rhodes,* pp. 169-171.
(2) C.O.291/53, pp. 180-1. Brynmor Jones to Havard, dated August 11, 1902.
(3) The London Convention signed on February 27, 1884, modified the terms of the Pretoria Convention of 1881 which had ended the first South African War. It contained certain new provisions for the protection of white alien residents in the Transvaal.
(4) C.O.417/338, pp. 400-2. Llwyd ap Iwan to Cecil Rhodes, dated September 30, 1901.
(5) Worsfold. *The Reconstruction of the New Colonies under Lord Milner,* Vol. 11, pp. 91-117.
(6) Crankshaw. *The Forsaken Idea,* Vol. II, p. 134.
(7) F.O.6/496, pp. 101-2. Lyttelton Gell to Lord Cranborne, dated October 28, 1901.
(8) *Ibid,* pp. 109-110. Lyttelton Gell to Norton, dated November 20, 1901.
(9) Lyttelton Gell MSS. Llwyd ap Iwan to Lyttelton Gell, dated October 29, 1901.
(10) *Ibid,* Thomas Rhys to Lyttelton Gell, dated February 23, 1901.
(11) *Ibid,* Mil 1/588. Lord Milner to Lyttelton Gell, dated March 23, 1902.
(12) F.O.6/496, pp. 198-201. Lyttelton Gell to Sir T. Sanderson, dated August 20, 1902.
(13) C.O.417/358, pp. 636-640. Carnegie Ross to Foreign Secretary, dated May 6, 1902. *See also* F.O.6/477, p. 3 May 6, 1902.
(14) In 1901, for instance, 125,951 immigrants reached the Argentine and 80,251 left it. The Welsh were obviously not the only people who wished to go elsewhere. (F.O.6/476, p. 60).
(15) By a later decree of the Government on January 28, 1903, a further drive was undertaken to make land available for settlers in Chubut. They were allowed individually to occupy 2500 hectares on favourable terms of credit, but undertook unreservedly to become Argentine citizens after two years. It is interesting that this decree authorized the executive to grant title deeds to the original Welsh settlers in the Andes valley. (F.O.6/480, pp. 80-2. Harford to the Foreign Office, dated February 11, 1903.
(16) F.O.6/496, pp. 210-12. W. M. Hughes to Chamberlain, dated June 24, 1902; and pp. 222-3. John G. Jones to Chamberlain, dated June 30, 1902.
(17) Chamberlain appears to have attached much importance to the report on Chubut written by Sir Thomas Holdich, who had visited the colony. The report, dated August 2, 1902, made it clear that if a scheme for emigration to South Africa could be sponsored, the majority of the settlers would welcome a return to the British flag. (F.O.6/496, pp. 173-192).
(18) The name of the Archdruid, as spelt in a newspaper report, dated June 27, 1902, was "Guty Ardroll" *(sic).* [Gutyn Ebrill].

(19) C.O.291/40, pp. 46 and 735. Milner to Chamberlain, dated July 13, 1902, and August 1, 1902.

(20) C.O.291/53, p. 179. August 7, 1902.

(21) See the notice on him in the *Dictionary of Welsh Biography,* p. 1001.

(22) A copy of Milner's reply was published in the *Liverpool Mercury,* June 16, 1902.

(23) C.O.291/53, pp. 853-58. Vaughan to the Colonial Office, dated September 24, 1902. This is the letter in which Vaughan detailed the whole course of his negotiations, as well as his grievances, prior to his final break with the department.

(24) Turner. *Mr. Buchan, Writer,* Chapter 3, pp. 37-41.

(25) Buchan. *The African Colony,* p. 272.

(26) C.O.291/53, pp. 853-58, as reported in Vaughan's letter to the Colonial Office, dated September 24, 1902.

(27) *Ibid,* pp. 180-1. Brynmor Jones to Havard, dated August 11, 1902.

(28) *Ibid,* pp. 188-193. Chamberlain to Milner, dated August 30, 1902.

(29) C.O.417/367, pp. 375-8. September 2, 1902.

(30) C.O.291/42, p. 525. Milner to Chamberlain, dated September 29, 1902.

(31) F.O.6/496, p. 242. Clarke to the Foreign Office, dated September 24, 1902. Another copy was sent by the South African Emigration Committee to O. M. Edwards, with the request to forward it to the Colonial Office. He did so, adding in his covering letter that he had complied with the request "because I know many of them and would be able to give information regarding them." (C.O.291/51, p. 445. O. M. Edwards to the Colonial Office, dated October 20, 1902).

(32) C.O.291/51, pp. 446-9. Memorial to Chamberlain, dated September 11, 1902.

(33) C.O.291/53, pp. 848-9. Vaughan to the Colonial Office, dated September 8 1902.

(34) *Ibid,* pp. 853-8. Vaughan to the Colonial Office, dated September 24, 1902.

(35) *Ibid,* pp. 851 and 868.

(36) *Ibid,* pp. 859-60. Vaughan to the Colonial Office, dated September 28, 1902.

(37) *Ibid,* p. 863. October 12, 1902.

(38) C.O.291/43, p. 917. Milner to Chamberlain, dated October 31, 1902.

(39) C.O.291/49, pp. 280-1. Milner to Chamberlain, dated December 15, 1902.

(40) C.O.291/53, pp. 867-8. J. A. Evans to the Mayor of Capetown, dated October 10, 1902, enclosed in Vaughan's letter to the Colonial Office, dated November 8, 1902.

(41) *Ibid,* pp. 865-6. Vaughan to the Colonial Office, dated November 8, 1902.

(42) He was later to write historical works and collaborate with Lord Howard de Walden in a play *The Children of Don.* Vaughan died on October 15, 1919, at the age of 56.

(43) C.O.291/48, pp. 365-8. Llwyd ap Iwan to Erasmus Jones, of Chubut, enclosed in the latter's letter to Clarke and forwarded in Clarke's despatch to the Foreign Office, dated November 25, 1902.

(44) *Ibid.*

(45) *Ibid,* pp. 48-56. Colonial Office to Milner, dated November 1, 1902.

(46) C.O.293/6. Reports 1903 (K.203).

(47) C.O.293/24. Reports 1905, p. Aa 1.

(48) C.O.291/63, enclosed in D. S. Jones's letter to Harford, dated August 12, 1903.

(49) *Ibid.*

(50) F.O.6/496, p. 273. Milner to Chamberlain by telegram, dated April 25, 1903.

(51) C.O.291/63. Harford to the Foreign Office, dated July 1, 1903.

(52) C.O.291/61. May 2, 1903.

(53) F.O.6/496, p. 286. Milner to Chamberlain, dated July 6, 1903.

(54) C.O.291/63. Harford to the Foreign Office, dated August 17, 1903.

(55) F.O.6/496, pp. 298-306. Harford to Larcom, dated August 19, 1903.

(56) C.O.291/63. Foreign Office to the Colonial Office, dated August 24, 1903.

(57) C.O.291/57. Milner to Chamberlain, dated June 6, 1903.

(58) C.O.291/61. May 23, 1903. The loan here mentioned was the Guaranteed Loan of £35,000,000 advanced by the British Government to cover the estimated deficit of the Transvaal in 1901-2, and meet the requirements of that colony in all its departments. Of this sum, £3,000,000 was set aside for the expenses of land settlement.

(59) C.O.291/63. John G. Jones to Hartord, dated August 8, 1903.

(60) *Ibid.* J. G. Jones to Harford, dated July 25, 1903. This was a copy of a letter which had been previously sent to Harford, but which had not arrived at its destination.

(61) *Ibid.* D. S. Jones to Harford, dated August 12, 1903.

(62) *Ibid.* John G. Jones to Harford, dated September 25, 1903.

(63) F.O.6/489, pp. 206-7. Letter from Harford, dated February 8, 1904.

(64) C.O.291/68. Milner to Lyttleton, dated January 25, 1904.

(65) F.O.6/489. Letter from Harford *op cit*

(66) C.O.291/78. W. O. Davies to Lyttleton, dated August 12, 1904.

(67) C.O.417/395. March 7, 1904.

(68) C.O.417/368, pp. 548-9. Owen Thomas to Lord Egerton of Tatton, dated April 16, 1902.

(69) Thomas had undertaken to compile this report at the request of the Rhodes Trustees who had paid him £500 for the work. The report was originally no more than 20 pages, and in order to expand it into a book, Thomas advertised for literary assistance. Frederick William Rolfe, *alias* Corvo, the eccentric author of *Hadrian VIII,* applied and was accepted by Thomas as his literary collaborator. Eventually the book was completed and published, and Rolfe received a fee of £50. Relations between the two men were amicable at first, but Rolfe, whose financial circumstances were a perpetual nightmare to him, chose to believe that he had not been fairly remunerated and decided to bring a legal action against Thomas. In August, 1904, a writ was issued against the latter, but the case did not come up for hearing until 1907. Rolfe claimed £2000 for the work he had done, and then whittled the sum down to £1000. Thomas, however, was able to reproduce sufficient evidence to invalidate the claim, and in January that year he obtained a favourable verdict with costs. *See* Weeks *Corvo,* pp. 214-3 and 257-8.

I am indebted to Mr. Tom Jaine of the Royal Commission on Historical Manuscripts for drawing my attention to the case of Rolfe *versus* Thomas.

(70) Lyttelton Gell MSS. Owen Thomas to R. J. Roberts, dated August 30, 1904.

(71) C.O.291/89. John G. Jones to G. R. Hughes, dated September 27, 1904, enclosed in a despatch from Haggard to the Marquess of Lansdowne, dated November 18, 1904.

(72) *Ibid.* John G. Jones to Haggard, dated September 27, 1904.

(73) C.O.291/80. Milner to Lyttleton, dated January 9, 1905.
(74) C.O. 293/24. Reports for 1905, p. LO 5.
(75) F.O.6/496. Haggard to the Foreign Office, dated August 1, 1905.

BIBLIOGRAPHY

(a) Original Sources

Public Record Office (PRO)

(1)   Foreign Office Records.

F.O.6   General Correspondence. Argentine Republic up to 1878. Nos. 254-351.

F.O.6   General Correspondence. Argentine Republic 1879-1905. Nos. 352-494.

F.O.6/496   Welsh Colony in Chubut.

F.O.5   General Correspondence. United States of America. Series 11, 1879-1905.

(2)   Colonial Office Records.

C.O.417   South Africa. Original Correspondence of High Commission, 1884-1925.

C.O.291   Transvaal. Correspondence Original. Secretary of State, 1877-1910.

C.O.680   Transvaal and Orange River Colony. Correspondence Register of Out Letters, 1901-2.

C.O.293   Transvaal Administration. Reports. Sessional Papers, 1880-1925.

C.O.679   Transvaal and Orange River Colony. Register of Correspondence, 1900-2.

C.O.45   Canada. Sessional Papers, 1764-1925.

C.O.42   Canada. Correspondence Original Secretary of State, 1700-1922.

National Library of Wales (NLW)

E.10816   Newspaper cuttings relating to the emigration from Chubut to Canada, 1902.

C.18427   Letters to Tobit Evans, 1885-1908.

Lyttelton Gell MSS in the possession of Mrs. A. E. Gell, O.B.E.

(b) Printed Work

An Official Handbook of Information relating to the Dominion of Canada, 1890.

BEERBOHN, Julius. Wanderings in Patagonia (London, 1879).

BOWEN, E. G. The Welsh Colony in Patagonia, 1865-1885 (Geographical Journal, Vol. 132, March 1966).

BUCHAN, John. The African Colony (London, 1903).

CRANKSHAW, Edward. The Forsaken Idea (London, 1952).

DIXIE, Lady Florence. Across Patagonia (London, 1880).

DAVIES, Alun. Michael Jones a'r Wladfa (Transactions of the Honourable Society of Cymrodorion, Pt. II, 1966).

Dictionary of Welsh Biography (London, 1953).

Economic Development of the Argentine Republic in the last fifty years. (Buenos Aires, 1919).

FERNS, H. S. Britain and Argentina in the nineteenth century. (Oxford, 1960).

GARCIA, M.R. Answer to Mr. MacDonnell (Paris, 1873).

Geographical Journal, 1966.

Geographical Magazine, October, 1961. Article by R. Bryn Williams on the Chubut colony.

HOLDICH, T. H. Countries of the King's Award (London, 1904).

HEADHAM, Cecil. The Milner Papers. South Africa, 1899-1905 (London, 1933).

JONES, Lewis. Cymru Newydd (Caernarvon, 1898).

Letters concerning the country of the Argentine Republic (London, 1869).

LOCKHART, J. G. and WOODHOUSE, Hon. C. M. Rhodes (London, 1963)

MUSTERS, G. Gh. At Home with the Patagonians (London, 1963).

MORENO, F. Notes preliminaires sur une excursion aux territoires de Newquen, Rio Negro, Chubut et Santa Cruz (La Plata, 1897).

MORTON, A. S. History of Prairie Settlement (Toronto, 1938).

McCOURT, E. Saskatchewan (Toronto, 1968).

Parliamentary Debates, 1899, 1901.

PINTO-DUSCHINSKY. Michael. The political thought of Lord Salisbury, 1854-68 (London, 1967).

PRICHARD, H. H. Through the heart of Patagonia (London, 1902).

Saskatchewan History (Saskatoon, 1948-).

South American Missionary Magazine (London, 1856-).

Tracts relating to Canada (1888-1893). Dominion of Canada; Manitoba and the North-West Territories. Report by P. R. Ritchie, 1892.

THOMAS, Lewis H. Lloyd George's visit to the North West, 1899. (Saskatchewan History, Vol. III, Winter 1950, No. 1).

TURNER, A. C. Mr. Buchan, Writer (London, 1949).

THOMAS, Owen. Agricultural and Pastoral Prospects of South Africa (London, 1904).

WILLIAMS, R. Bryn. Y Wladfa (Cardiff, 1962).

WRENCH, J. E. Alfred, Lord Milner (London, 1958).

WRIGHT, J. F. C. Saskatchewan. This History of a Province (McClelland & Steward, 1955).

WORSFOLD, W. B. The Reconstruction of the New Colonies under Lord Milner (London, 1913).

WEEKS, Donald. Corvo (London, 1971).

INDEX

Hughes, W. M., of Chubut.
 writes to Chamberlain, 105.
 106.

Ionian, The.
 advance party of Chubut Welsh sail to
 Canada in, 84.
Indians, 9, 13.
 successful raids by, 16, 18.
 relations between Chubut Welsh and,
 17, 18, 31, 32.
 Argentine Government's offensive
 against, 23, 31.
 Llwyd ap Iwan's strange statement on,
 100.
Iriqoyen, Dr, Argentine Minister of the
 Interior, 35.
Irrigation, 23, 24, 26, 37, 39, 43, 65, 72,
 99, 105, 120, 124, 125, 130, 131, 132.

Johannesburg, 108, 112, 118, 134.
Jones, D. Brynmor, M.P.
 deputed to meet Foreign Office on
 behalf of Chubut delegates, 49.
 sends Memorial containing alternative policies for Chubut to Foreign
 Office, 49.
 his question in House of Commons on
 Trelew arrests, 52.
 favours emigration from Chubut to
 South Africa, 99.
 recommends Vaughan to Colonial
 Office, 110.
Jones, D. S., of Chubut.
 made President of South African
 Emigration Committee, 113.
 chosen to visit South Africa, 118.
 dissatisfied with proposals of Transvaal Government, 121, 122, 125.
 returns to Chubut, 123.
Jones, Evan E., former Chubut colonist,
 82.
Jones, John G., of Chubut.
 writes to Chamberlain, 105.
 accepts conditions of Transvaal
 Government on behalf of Chubut
 Welsh, 136.
Jones, Lewis.
 negotiates with Argentine Government, 18, 19, 20.
 his interview with MacDonnell, 19.

accepts conditions imposed by Argentine Government, 21.
appointed *Alcade* in Chubut, 21.
appeals for more Welsh emigrants, 22.
rejects offer to be Vice-Consul at
Chubut, 28.
appointed Commissioner at Chubut
for Argentine Government, 28.
dismissed from his post, 32.
imprisoned in Buenos Aires, 33.
36, 37, 40, 48.
British Government rejects his
application to be Vice-Consul at
Chubut, 42.
editor of *Y Drafod,* 43.
ruined by floods, 53.
Jones, Michael D., Principal of Bala
College.
7, 11, 22, 81, 89.
his letter to MacDonnell, 22.
his appeal for more emigrants to
Chubut, 23.
Jones, William, M.P.
his appeal to Chamberlain, 72.

La Nacion, of Buenos Aires.
prints O'Donnell's article on
Education in Welsh, 44.
56.
Langton Grange, The.
Chubut delegates sail to South Africa
in, 119.
130.
Lewis, Gwilym, former Chubut settler.
his appeal to Chamberlain, 73.
Lewis, William, Secretary to Emigration
Movement Committee in Chubut, 57.
Liverpool, 83, 84, 85, 86.
advance party of Chubut Welsh sail to
Canada from, 84, 90.
farewell reception organized for
Chubut Welsh in, 89.
Llewelyn, Sir John, Chairman of Welsh
Patagonian Committee, 89, 94.
Lloyd George, David, M.P.
visits North-West Territories of
Canada, 60.
Lloyd Jones, Rev. D., of Chubut, 66.
attacks emigration from Chubut to
Canada, 86.

Paraguay.
joins with Argentine in war against Uruguay, 15.
Patagonia, 7, 8, 14, 20, 27, 33, 39, 53, 71, 73, 80, 81, 82, 83, 84, 89, 98, 99, 105.
Argentine Government's anxiety to establish sovereignty over, 9, 13.
American Welsh views on emigration to, 23, 24.
proposed new Welsh settlements in, 25, 41.
appeal that it be declared British territory, 45.
Phillips, T. Benbow.
sent as delegate to seek intervention of British Government, 45.
46, 48, 51, 60, 65, 98.
received at Foreign Office, 49.
Port Madryn.
construction of railway between Chubut and, 37.
38, 47, 64, 66, 85, 87, 106, 124.
Preston, T. R., Inspector of Canadian Agencies in Europe.
criticises *Times* article on state-aided emigration, 61.
Pretoria.
negotiations between Chubut delegates and Transvaal Government at, 119, 120, 130.

Rawson, Senor, Argentine Minister of the Interior, 8, 12, 27.
his motives in promoting Welsh colony at Chubut, 9, 12, 13.
his proposal regarding Falkland Islands to British Government, 10.
provides relief for Chubut Welsh, 13.
British Government's tribute to, 13.
resigns his post, 15.
Rawson, 15, 40, 41(2), 48, 55, 65, 79.
ruined by floods, 53.
Rees, W. J., of Swansea, agent of Canadian Government, 58, 81, 97.
visits North-West Territories of Canada, 60.
visits Chubut, 64.
explains situation in Chubut to Chamberlain, 72, 73.
Rhodes, Cecil.

Llwyd ap Iwan's letter to, 98.
Rhodesia.
proposal that Chubut Welsh should settle in, 101, 103, 134, 135, 138.
Rhys, Thomas, professor at Bala-Bangor College.
favours emigration from Chubut to South Africa, 81, 82, 102.
his correspondence with Lyttelton Gell, 81, 102.
criticises Welsh Patagonian Committee and Griffith, 82.
Ricciardi, former Boer leader.
involved in establishing Boer colony in Chubut, 104.
Richards, Rev. David, chaplain of H.M.S. *Flora.*
his statement on desire of Chubut Welsh to emigrate, 57.
62.
Rio Negro, 9, 12, 27, 31, 79.
Indians control land between Chubut and, 16.
Roberts, R. J., of Chubut.
chosen to visit South Africa, 118.
dissatisfied with proposals of Transvaal Government, 121, 122, 125.
returns to Chubut, 123.
Owen Thomas's letter to, 135.
Roca, General, President of the Argentine Republic, 27, 31, 55, 66.
effects of his colonizing policy on Chubut colony, 28.
visits Chubut, 46, 48.
Rumbold, Sir Horace, British Minister in Buenos Aires.
recommends Lewis Jones as Vice-Consul, 28.
Rush, The.
Welsh emigrants sail from New York to Patagonia in, 23.
abandoned by emigrants at Montevideo, 24.

St. James's Gazette.
criticises Chamberlain's refusal to help Chubut Welsh, 76.
Salisbury, Robert Gascoyne-Cecil, 3rd Marquess of, Secretary for Foreign Affairs.

rejects proposal for appointment of
Vice-Consul at Chubut, 39, 42.
his attitude towards Memorial presented by Chubut delegates, 46.
48, 49(2).

Saltcoats, Saskatchewan, Canada.
Chubut Welsh choose to settle in, 91.
criticism of settlement at, 93.

Santa Cruz, River.
proposal to settle Chubut colonists
near, 25.

Santa Fe, province of, 14.
raided by Indians, 16.
some Chubut colonists leave for, 17.

South Africa.
British Government and emigration to,
40, 57, 74, 76, 77.
58, 61, 66, 81, 82, 93.
Chamberlain's partiality to, 77.
campaign for emigration from Chubut
to, 97.
reasons for failure of plans for settlement of Chubut Welsh in, 124, 125,
130.

South Africa Company, 81, 98, 100, 101.
South African Emigration Committee.
See Emigration Movement Committee.
Spriggs, Sir Gordon, Cape Prime
Minister, 108.
Standard, The, of London.
comments on Chubut Welsh, 69.
Standard, The, English newspaper
circulating in Buenos Aires.
its comment on internal situation in
Argentine, 16.
55.

Tarnassi, Senor, an Italian lawyer.
his scheme for Italian colony in
Chubut, 53, 54.
Tejidor, Senor, Argentine Minister for
Foreign Affairs, 18.
Tello, Senor, Governor of Chubut, 43.
Terra del Fuego, 31.
Thomas, Alfred, M.P., Chairman of
Welsh Parliamentary Party.
deputed to meet Foreign Office on
behalf of Chubut delegates, 49.
his appeal to Chamberlain, 72.

Thomas, D. A., M.P.
provokes Chamberlain in the House of
Commons, 78.
Thomas, Rev. J. Ll., Vicar of Aber-
pergwm.
suggests name for Welsh settlement at
Saltcoats, 94.
Thomas, Owen, later General Sir.
his early career, 133.
critical of Lord Milner, 134.
advocates Chubut emigration to
Rhodesia, 134.
his report on South Africa and
Rhodesia, 134, 135.
Thomas, T. M., of Chubut.
leads expedition to Andes, 39.
Thornton, Edward, British Minister in
Buenos Aires.
Rawson communicates his proposal
on Falkland Islands to, 10.
Times, The.
favours state-aided emigration, 61.
Transvaal, 57, 61, 97, 98, 99, 102, 105,
116, 118, 119, 127, 134.
Chubut delegates receive proposals
from Government of, 120, 121.
drawbacks of settlement in, 121, 125,
132, 134.
dispute over River Vaal between Cape
Colony and, 124, 130.
counter-proposals of Chubut delegates not acceptable to, 131.
Chubut Welsh accept proposals of
Government of, 136.
Trelew.
arrest of Welsh colonists at, 48, 52.
Argentine troops at, 54.
the case of John Morley of, 55, 56.
65, 79.
celebration of Edward VII's
coronation organized at, 106.

Uruguay.
hostilities between Argentine and, 15,
16.
United States of America.
Welsh emigrants leave for Chubut
from, 22, 23.
outbreak of anti-English feeling
amongst Welsh in, 23, 24.